FROM THE JORDAN TO THE SEA

A CHRISTIAN RESPONSE TO ISRAEL'S WAR

MICHAEL J. SUTTON

DEDICATION

To the children.
May they never see war.
May they live in peace.

CONTENTS

ACKNOWLEDGMENTS

To the gutless, faithless, spineless, cowardly Christian leaders, pastors, priests, ministers, bishops, and archbishops, academics, influencers, celebrities, and journalists, who are silent on Israel, on Gaza, on war, on genocide, too busy with their kingdoms on earth, their investments, properties, wealth and power, without your apostasy, your moral and spiritual bankruptcy, this book could not have been written.

1.

WHO IS RESPONSIBLE FOR ISRAEL'S WAR?

Israel is at war, again.

In this conflict, a few features stand out for me. What are they? In September 2024, Israel planted bombs on thousands of communication devices which exploded in Lebanon killing many and injuring thousands.

Israel has been assassinating political leaders around the region especially in Gaza, including over one hundred journalists, cultural leaders, doctors, and so on. Their war also targets schools, mosques, hospitals and churches. Their war has razed Gaza to the ground, making over two million people homeless.

Israel has been engaged in genocide in Gaza ostensibly because of the horrors of October 7 last year. One estimate is that over 40,000 people in Gaza, including around 11,000 children have been killed. As in all war, the real number will be much higher. It is urban warfare, and over 200,000 buildings have been levelled, so the real death toll will be catastrophic. The Lancet estimate is that 186,000 deaths have resulted from this conflict. This estimate seems more accurate.

Israel has used propaganda, social media, and apologists to minimize the effects of war and downplay casualties. A common argument is that casualty rates cannot be trusted as they come from the Gaza Health Ministry. Another argument is that, by algorithms and formulae, the death toll ratio in this war is really low compared with other conflicts, and that the Israeli military is going out of its way to reduce collateral damage. These hypotheses, often presented as truth, are just devices of state propaganda, widely accepted by Israeli sympathizers in the West.

Israel has a sophisticated network of media organizations around the world which advances their perspective for various reasons. Many commentators, analysts and journalists are apologists for genocide. Many Christians active online, including 'independent' journalists on the Far-Right, Alt-right, and Republican side of American politics believe God is on the side of Israel.

As for Israel, there is no endgame in their war, except the slogan of 'From the Jordan to the Sea,' a vision of Greater Israel, which necessities genocide in several nations, in order to achieve a largely dubious geographical expansion which will not be recognized by the global community.

These are, as I see them, the basic brushstrokes of

the character of this war. I would argue that this war is a consequence of Israeli identity. I would go as far as to say that it is inevitable. In other words, it was bound to happen, not that it was unavoidable, but given a choice, Israel, as it exists, doesn't want peace. Israel wants war.

The Israelis don't enjoy peace and probably never will. They have been constantly at war with their neighbors since 1948. The reasons for this are complex, complicated, and contested. I feel for everyone involved in this conflict, on all sides. The whole Israeli/Palestinian debacle is a tragedy of the modern era.

We are all responsible for this mess, morally and spiritually. The failure for Israel to find peace is the failure of the world and if we cannot find a way forward here, then there is no hope anywhere. Three major world religions intersect this conflict, and they all claim to be from God, and are all children under the covenant of Abraham and yet, despite everything, peace is elusive.

To be honest, I have no idea what the answer is. It certainly is not, 'From the Jordan to the Sea,' or 'From the River to the Sea.' It must have something to do with our hearts and our attitudes to others made in the image of God. If we can see others as people whom God endowed with his identity, and people whom God loves, as he loves us, perhaps this is a way forward, but will there be lasting peace? I don't know. I am not convinced that it is possible given that so much blood has been shed, and the logic of vengeance and payback and retribution is so compelling.

I lost my father to an accident, and it was gut-wrenching. I cannot imagine losing him to war, or an Israeli bomb, or sniper's bullet, all in the sickening context of 'well, it was acceptable because we need to get rid of Hamas.'

It would not be acceptable to me. I don't have children, and I am not married, but to have my wife and children killed by an army bent on killing others would not make me a lover of peace. I would lose my mind in grief, and my entire moral code would be shaken. If war came to my street and every house was destroyed, then I am sure that an anger would grip me, and a hatred would overcome me. If my entire suburb was levelled and the local hospital was bombed and the doctors were executed ward by ward because one of them might have been a terrorist, the desire for revenge would overwhelm me. There but for the grace of God go I, but I don't know what I would do.

Those hypocrites in Australia who tell Palestinians to 'shut up and forgive Israel' still hate the Japanese for what happened over 80 years ago in the jungles of Malaya. These hypocrites who tell Palestinians to forgive Israel hate migrants and aborigines. I know, I have read many of their articles. They are racist bigots with a façade of the Christian faith, largely cultural Christians of the Far-Right. There is a whole industry now of Christian 'media commentary' in Australia, and it is full of hate. There are very few ethnic groups these new so-called 'Christian journalists' do not hate. The Australian church is also full of these hypocrites who tell Palestinians to forgive Israel, but will not practice forgiveness themselves, or acceptance or love. The attitude of the Australian Christian church reminds me of the words of Jesus when he called out hypocrites in Matthew 7: 1-5.

'Do not judge, or you too will be judged. For in the same way you judge others, you will be judged, and with the measure you use, it will be measured to you. Why do you look at the speck of sawdust in your brother's eye and pay no attention to the plank in your own eye? How can you say to your brother, 'Let me take the speck out of your eye,' when all the time there is a plank in your own eye? You hypocrite, first take the plank out of your own eye, and then you will see clearly to remove the speck from your brother's eye.'

Israel has been involved in at least two major wars, the war preceding the establishment of the state of Israel, and the 1967 war. This third war seems to be the effort to realize the controversial vision of Greater Israel, 'From the Jordan to the Sea.' For many Israelis this is the goal of their nationalist project and pours cold war on the notion that Israel is simply exacting justice for October 7, 2023. That is a complete fabrication.

This war is clearly about redefining geographical borders and expanding the territory of Israel, to encompass Gaza, the West Bank, Lebanon, and Iran, at least, for now. The goal is partly a real estate bonanza, under the American shield, and entails sending millions of Palestinians into the desert, into refugee camps, so the prime coastal properties of Gaza can be rezoned into beautiful, expensive beachfront property for the filthy rich.

All nations have goals and projects, aspirations and ambitions, but the measure of a state is how they care for their population, and it is clear that Israel is not only an Apartheid state, but unlike South Africa, there is no hope for the future, only blood, and lots of it. There have been so many lies around October 7, 2023, and yet, despite being debunked, they are still used to justify war, and to demonize the Palestinians as people worthy of death.

As soon as the chaos and death of October 7 became clear, Netanyahu and his confederates invoked the strangest of all ancient tribal stories, the divine instructions from the prophet Samuel to the first monarch of the 12 tribes of Israel, Saul, to massacre the entire clan of Amalekites. This ancient story, largely dismissed as fiction today, even by most Jewish people, is a call to institute tribal laws around payback, retribution, and revenge, principles alien to any modern nation-state, repugnant to the ideals of democracy, freedom, and human rights, and antithetical to the Geneva Conventions. Only a fool would think that the logic of payback is one-sided. Modernity has struggled to expunge, exorcise, and expel the evil logic of payback, but that fool Netanyahu, talks about curses and blessings, and has let the genie out of the bottle, staining humanity in the vile rhetoric of the politics of revenge and the divine will.

As a Christian and follower of Jesus, the teachings of Christ, would act as a counterbalance to the awful evils of war. If the Gaza War came to my middle-class suburb, as it has in the Middle East, there would be an intense struggle in my inner being. This would play out in my response to war, even war inflicted upon myself and my family. There is no Christian teaching advocating revenge, payback or retribution. This is in contrast to the Hebrew Bible, which is all about revenge, both human and divine. The failure of the Old Testament to deal with sin is the reason for God to send his Messiah to deal with the power, the penalty and the guilt of sin. Christians believe that Jesus is the presence, the power, and the person of God. By his life, death and resurrection Jesus shows us that love, not hate, is God's answer to the world.

Christians believe that it was with the coming of Jesus that the logic of revenge was overcome by the love of God by sending into the Son the wrath of God so that God himself placed upon the Son the sin of the world, including revenge. As Christians, we believe in the power of God's Spirit who enables us to love, encourages us to love, and exhorts us to love.

Sadly, most Christian commentary on Israel, on October 7 and on the history of the Middle East is composed by many fake Christians who neither know God, nor love him. They are a disgrace. They mispresent God and they misrepresent the good news of Jesus. I also call my own people to account, those in Australia. In Australia, America's colony in the Asia Pacific, most online Christian 'news' agencies are pro-Israeli, and other views are ignored, condemned, or silenced. These Australian Christian apologists for genocide are falling over each other in an effort to show America their loyalty to Christian Zionism. They are penning some of the most extreme anti-Palestinian hit pieces, with a rhetoric and vitriol that should be of grave concern to authorities.

Many of these authors hold to the same Premillennial 'end times' theology as the three Australians who, in cold blood, shot and killed several police officers who turned up at their farm on 12 December 2022, in Australia's first act of Christian terrorism. Far from being marginalized, this fundamentalist theology is flourishing Down Under, as many await the 'Rapture,' when they believe Jesus will take them to all to heaven

I have outlined the basic character of Israel's current war, and yet I fear that on one level it is not about Israel at all, but what is happening in Gaza, in Jerusalem, in Lebanon, and in Iran is the template for

World War 3, which is upon us. I grieve for the children of Jerusalem, Lebanon, Gaza, Israel, and Iran, and for those in Yemen, the Sudan, Ukraine and Russia. Yet these conflicts are but the first sign of dark clouds on the horizon. War with China is coming and perhaps nuclear war between America and Russia, and I weep for us all.

What will be the character of WW3? The template for WW3 has already been provided to us by Israel's new war. The applications are virtually a simple extension and extrapolation. First, all forms of technology are potential weapons. This includes drones, phones, pagers, computers, tablets, cars, everything.

Second, political leaders, journalists, cultural leaders, doctors, nurses, and first responders will be the first to die in war. Their deaths will be justified by statements in media and governments such as 'beneath this hospital is a terror cell.' The UN Declaration on Human Rights is not worth the paper it is written on. All bets are off.

Third, genocide is now accepted by the West, and I am not talking about governments. I am talking about people in general. The greatest threat to world peace is the American middle class. America will destroy Taiwan and hope to destroy China. They will bomb Beijing and other major cities and millions will die. Their deaths will be widely accepted in the West as 'necessary.' Some say that most victims in Gaza were those involved with Hamas. This means that the deaths of 11,000 children were justified because their parents were in the wrong political organization. They will say the same thing about war with China, except the numbers of the dead will be much higher. The enemies of China will say, 'well, these 2 million were all people related to or involved in the terrorist organization called the Chinese Communist Party.' This will include the children and the women, guilt by association. This logic justifies genocide and America, and the West will applaud.

Fourth, propaganda will be used to minimize the effects of war and downplay casualties. Those who refuse to fight or refuse to support WW3 will be put in prison or killed. Social media will be restricted, and the West will implement wartime legislation to control the entire population. In Australia, they already have the Bio-Security Act, and will have the Misinformation Act, and a few others to create their war society. I call it fascism because fascism is the inevitable result of representative democracy just as tyranny is the product of unrestrained autocracy. Unfortunately, we have been dealt a hand from a stacked deck of cards.

Fifth, sophisticated network of media around the world will advance, assist, collaborate and defend America's war to stop history. Many journalists, celebrities and political leaders will be apologists for genocide.

Who is responsible for WW3? It is America. It is not Russia, China, or Iran. The culprit and the one remembered by history will be America. The goal is to keep America strong and to remake the world with an American face. All nations must bow to America in humble adoration, and if they don't, they will be sent back to the Stone Age. The enemy of freedom is not Anthony Fauci, or the World Health Organization or the World Economic Forum or the United Nations, but America, the nation which craves to be the new global empire, a singular power. As I wrote in 'World War 3, Will you stand for peace?' (Hidden Riad

Publishing, 2024), the goal is to create chaos everywhere, so the world burns except for America and its allies. Only nations bowing to America will be allowed to survive. The 'free' nations will thrive with America at the center. The rest of the world will be a wasteland.

Making American Great Again entails the destruction of any nation which dares to challenge American power or coexist independently. History is against America, but they are the spoilers. The thinking, 'if we can't be number 1, then no one can.' America, if it is playing any role in the New Testament, is Babylon.

I would argue that WW3 is a consequence of human identity. I would go as far as to say that it is inevitable. Even if this is the case, standing for freedom and standing for peace is still the only way forward out of the madness.

This book is the sequel to *'World War 3: Will you Stand for Peace?'* In this book, I present ten reflections on Israel's war composed from September to October 2024. I include two reflections (chapters 10 and 11) written following October 7, 2023. These two chapters were originally published in 2023 in my book *'The Lies, Lessons and Legacies of Covid Hysteria.'* Chapter 12 comes from my classic Freedom Matters Today series, written in 2022, and was originally published in *'Following Jesus when the Church has lost its way.'*

I seek to provide a Christian perspective, because I believe in God and I believe I must stand before God one day and give an account of my life, and what I have done, and what I have left undone. I want to stand before God with a clear conscience, and I want him to know that I did my best to promote the peace of God which I believe is found in Jesus.

At the end of the day, there can be common ground, and there must be if we wish to survive on this small blue planet. There must be mutual respect for mutual coexistence. If not, there is no hope for humanity, and if some part of humanity survives WW3, the world will be completely different.

If you want to see the future of New York or London, or Sydney, look at Gaza today. It is a mirror to our future. If you think it will not happen in your country, think again. On February 21, 2022, that delusion is what the people of Ukraine believed. On October 6, 2023, thousands of young people decided to go to a rock concert near the border with Gaza and the 250 hostages went about their lives unaware that many of them would never return home. On 6 October, 186,000 people in Gaza thought that they would live out their lives, albeit in an apartheid state. On November 28, 1947, who would have imagined that the UN Partition Plan for Palestine the following day, would have facilitated the nightmarish civil war which led to the creation of the state of Israel about six months later on May 14, 1948.

In war, no one is exempt, and we now have the technology to wage a brutal and unforgiving war, far from the public gaze, we are able to censor and restrict information, and cover up atrocities, and we are able to hit anyone at any time, without mercy, and this is the world we have created for ourselves.

'From the Jordan to the Sea,' is one slogan for one ambition, for one nation and yet all slogans have a weakness, for they are our creations, with our expectations, our designs and our hopes, and as such, they are not from God. 'From the Jordan to the Sea,' or 'From the river to the soil,' are slogans for people committed to the theology of the soil, the idea that God is a tribal deity, that place matters more than person, and that God is the god of geography. It is just land, it is just soil, it is just dirt. The world is full of dirt, the world is full of soil, and 8 billion make their home here. I believe in the God of revelation is more interested in people than place. The vision of God is for all of his creation, not only little corner of it. As Paul says in the Acts of the Apostles (13: 47).

> 'For this is what the Lord has commanded us: 'I have made you a light for the Gentiles, that you may bring salvation to the ends of the earth.''

If a Christian takes up the slogans of this conflict, they are selling God short, they are selling God out, and they are selling out the gospel, but millions of Christians worldwide have given up the good news and instead are preaching the nationalist vision of Greater Israel. It is not Christianity. It is not good news. It gives God the middle finger.

> *'To the ends of the earth' is our slogan. The good news, to the ends of the earth. A loving God, to the ends of the earth. True peace, and forgiveness, to the ends of the earth. Reconciliation to God, to the ends of the earth. A resurrected Savior and a living Lord to the ends of the earth.*

Despite the anger, the pain, the desire for revenge, God always tells us there is another way, and yet this is not a time for God, and it is not a time to listen to him, or obey, and if it is not, then how can we expect to stand in his presence when we so resolutely, defiantly, and stubbornly stand against him. It means we are on our own, and even though we quote him, and tell ourselves that he supports our way, and blesses our anger, and sanctifies our version of justice, it is not God, for we stand alone.

2.

WHAT IS THE TRUTH ABOUT ISRAEL'S WAR?

I am sure you have all seen the footage of the Iranian ballistic missiles raining out of the heavens in the night sky onto military targets in Israel. It is an image that is unforgettable, like a scene from a movie. For millions of Christians around the world, this event is evidence that the Rapture is coming soon, that, with the blink of an eye, all followers of Jesus will be taken into heaven. Not surprisingly, millions are ecstatic, excited, and expectant. For them, the end is nigh. But is it? What is really going on in the Middle East? What is the truth about the Israel-Iran War?

We are lucky to see these pictures at all. These days, corporations and the state censor most images and videos from Ukraine, Gaza, Yemen, Lebanon, and other war zones unless they fit the narrative. We can watch the bombing of Israel because the state wants us to sympathize with the Israelis and hate Iran.

If we saw the bombing of Gaza, we would be stunned, sickened and shocked, but they want to keep these images from us. America, Australia, and other friends of Israel want to manipulate us so they can channel our rage only along the approved narrative. Churches are also largely complicit in this agenda.

In a world of nation states, morality is only relevant if it suits the strategic national interest. Good and evil are categories absent in international relations. Morality is subordinate to strategic state interests. The truth is irrelevant. What does this mean?

In practice, it means that the war is important because it is a battle in America's long-term military ambitions in the region, to secure long-term access to oil resources for the American state in its upcoming war with China. That is the strategic goal, a resource grab for war, nothing more. Everything else is meaningless rhetoric.

But in our decadent, declining democracy, having the population onside is important, and so it is vital to control the information, and ensure that only the correct truth is revealed.

I have seen much of the footage and many of these ballistic missiles hit their targets. Despite this, the media corporations tell us that the attack was a failure, even though we can see with our own eyes what happened. I know what I saw. When a yellow light hits the ground and there is an explosion, this means that a missile or projectile has reached the ground. Now, we are told, it is fake news. The media reports about the Iranian missiles reminds me of the American reporter during the George Floyd protests telling the audience that the protest was peaceful but behind him, everything was on flames.

Contrary to what many Christians believe, Israel is not an independent, sovereign state. It is an American puppet regime, an outpost, a colony, call it what you like, but it is firmly entrenched in the American imperialist project. Without America, there would be no Israel, certainly not in its current form. There would be peace in the region.

America protects Israel to secure long-term access to resources. That's it. That's all. That is the only reason for this alliance, oil. It is the only reason America even knows about the Middle East, oil, not democracy, and not freedom.

When we talk about media culpability, what do we mean here? Part of it is inherited political culture. Many truly believe that America rules by divine right, or fate, or is the defender of truth, liberty, and justice. If evidence to the contrary appears, they simply ignore it. That is the default factory setting of journalism. Class is important, as is gender, as is age, and national political culture, and nationalism. Once again, these filters trump morality. The life of a Palestinian, for example, is next to nothing, but the life of an Israeli, or an American, is priceless.

If the Israelis bomb a hospital, the media, if they report it at all, will use talking points that seem to sound very much like memos from Israel, that behind the hospital, or under the hospital was a terrorist organization. End of story. Therefore, the death toll is acceptable because after all, the goal is the kill the terrorist, no matter the human cost. The media will call it a humanitarian disaster, or an accident, or unfortunate incident. Nothing to see here.

But if the attack is reversed, if it is Iran doing the bombing or any enemy of America, then it is an act of terrorism, an evil act, and unprovoked aggression. If you raise the death toll with journalists or state proxies, you will get blank stares or denials, but they simply don't care and are cavalier about human life. Some are bought and paid for, some are too scared, but most will not care. Many truly believe that the value of human life is relative, not absolute, and even in this post-modern society, some lives are priceless, and others are of no value.

It is only the state, state institutions and proxies that engage in misinformation. People never do, they don't possess the organization, the ligaments of power or orchestration. The Australian state's 'Misinformation Bill' proposal is not in the Constitution so can be repealed by the next parliament. The Bill is designed to promote misinformation by the state against its own people. The Bill is to prepare the nation for war with China and this Act of Parliament will be used to censor the truth about the conflict and punish anyone who is interested in knowing the truth or anyone declaring the truth.

The state must know, by now, the cost of war with China, and it is catastrophic. This means that many in the state are complicit in expectant genocide and mass murder, for that is what a war with China will entail. The Misinformation Bill, along with the fascist Bio-Security Act is designed to murder Australian democracy and kill freedom, while promoting America's war against China, a war we will most certainly lose.

These mechanisms of misinformation are state disciplines on the production and dissemination of information, and what they mean is that we are already at war. States know that war is an awful thing,

ity is shaped to fit the story the state wants us to accept. It is not new. It has been around for decades. We saw this in the War on Terror. We saw this in Covid Hysteria. We see it in the War in Ukraine. We see it in the genocide in Gaza. Reality is simply an interpretation of facts molded, shaped, and curated. It is not a question of truth, but reimagined reality, so that what we remember is not what happened. We are told what we need to know, which is never the truth.

The American state, its puppet Israel, and its proxies around the world make sure the message is right. Is the state evil? Is this intentional? Is there moral responsibility. I would argue it is rather complicated, for states behave according to a set of principles. These principles compel them to act, and if they do not act in this way, the system repudiates them, or replaces them, or the actions of the state create a revolution so that the entire system collapses. This is unlikely, and unusual, but it does happen.

The beneficiaries of the imperialist state are the corporations, the financial interests and business in general. They control the state. Big finance, the war industry, and the old oligarchy of corporate power run governments, and always have in capitalism. Talking about the 'corporate takeover' of America, for example, is not alleging a conspiracy, but simply explaining the nature of a nation-state and 'how the system works.' Diplomats, bureaucrats, are simply salespeople for corporate power.

18

The reimagined reality is tailored to fit the audience, so they are dulled to what is happening in the Middle East, so it doesn't upset them at the dinner table, so it doesn't distract them from their TV shows, so it doesn't interrupt the sport. People in the West want to drive their cars, eat their food, and enjoy their life. They want cheap oil, they want low inflation, they want their welfare state. It is a middle-class dream. But it doesn't come cheap. The price is high. The price is blood. Lots of it. They say that when the crusaders overran Palestine in the Siege of Jerusalem in 1099, the streets were knee-deep in the blood of Muslims and Jews. Even today, it is awful to read of this terrible event. History has, however, not fully appreciated the indifference, callousness, and narcissism of the middle-class in America and modern Europe.

The American middle-class doesn't care about genocide in Gaza, or war in Yemen, or conflict in the Sudan. The middle-class doesn't care about the fall of Iran, or Lebanon, nor will it care when America bombs Beijing, and carpet bombs cities, killing millions of people. If Americans can get their cheap oil, keep their status, and maintain their prosperity, the world can burn.

What is the Christian response to the Iran-Israel War? First, talk about this war with your Christian friends, raise it in your church, bring it up in prayers, and listen to others and their perspectives. Present a Christian perspective. Be on the lookout for all the signs of an indoctrinated person, and a compromised institution. Beware of those who claim to be Christian and then tell you that killing others made in God's image is God's will.

Second, come out and be separate (2 Corinthians 6:

17). Leave your church, leave your denomination, leave your tradition and follow Jesus. Many churches are simply part of the imperialist state, they derive benefits, legitimacy and power from the state, and quite simply, are controlled by the state. Like what is happening in China, many churches in the West are state-controlled churches, though the instruments, the mechanisms, and the algorithms of control are more subtle. The church is simply another actor in the manufacturing of misinformation. You are in spiritual peril, and in great danger. Your eternal soul is of no concern to these churches. Their kingdom of money and power is opposed to the kingdom of God.

Gather with others of a like mind whenever, wherever. Your faith must be of relevance to the world around you, so if you are told by the church to 'shut up and pray,' or you are told, 'this is a complex issue,' or your legitimate questions about Israel's war are met with your condemnation, then you are in spiritual danger, so leave as soon as possible. You are, unfortunately, in a government-controlled church.

Third, read the New Testament for yourself. You do not need the priest or pastor to interpret the Bible to you. God speaks to all through his Word. You do not need your priest or pastor to validate your morality, conscience, or sense of justice. In the past, the clergy used to weep over sin, but these days, it seems the eyes of many are dry, and if these people are not weeping for the children of Gaza, Israel, Yemen, Sudan, Ukraine and Russia, then your pastor or priest is a minister not of God, but of diabolos, for if he does not weep for them, he will not weep for you.

Fourth, keep the eyes of your heart open. The message you hear on Sunday is most likely not the gospel. It is not about the kingdom of God. You are being actively lied to. You are part of an imperialist system where your religion is subordinate to the interests of the state. Your Jesus is a man whose identity is subordinate to the power of the state. Your faith is one that is subordinate to the ambitions of the state.

Fifth, remember, we are in the beginning of World War 3. State indoctrination and propaganda are working overtime to keep us in line, so we support the war, which is to guarantee long-term access to mineral resources in a war with China and Russia.

Sixth, avoid any church that is deeply concerned with public morality, in other words, the externals, for they are not followers of Christ. God is concerned with the heart. What is public morality? These days the church is obsessed with sex, gender, and reproduction. That's it. They don't care about war, suffering, or poverty. They never talk about the heart, and they certainly don't want you to think for yourself. They talk about 'family values,' or the good old days, or their reimagined history. Jesus was interested in the heart of a person, for out of the heart comes good and evil. It is impossible for a Christian to actively hate another person with unrelenting vigor, for it means the Spirit has no power, and that person has no life.

Seventh, remember that Christianity has no part with American imperialism or any imperialism. We follow Jesus, we do not follow Ceasar. We do not align ourselves with their war, their mass murder, or their message. To stand for freedom is a hard place to stand but stand you must. If you need encouragement, remember the words of Jesus in Matthew 7: 13-14.

'Enter through the narrow gate. For wide is the gate and broad is the road that leads to destruction, and many enter through it. But small is the gate and narrow the road that leads to life, and only a few find it.'

For the fruit of the Spirit includes love, and today, with the Iran-Israel war, you see only hate in many churches who have lost their way, lost their love, and lost their Lord.

3.

HOW MANY MUST DIE FOR PEACE?

In September 2024, Israel, armed with American-made bombs and missiles, expanded its war of aggression against Lebanon and Iran, threatening to plunge the entire region into a mad world of blood, death, and slaughter. In October 2024, the Israeli Prime Minister announced that if Lebanon does not destroy Hezbollah, then Israel will destroy Lebanon as it has destroyed Gaza. America and its allies will support Israel, no matter the death toll to civilians. The Christian church in the West, likewise, will stand by and do nothing, for it is also largely complicit in every action taken by America.

Netanyahu wants to associate himself with the likes of Pol Pot, Stalin, and Attila the Hun as a mass murderer of innocent people. Ah, yes, he has his reasons, all murderers do. They all have their schemes, and their justifications, and their rationale, but they are just mass murderers, plain and simple.

October 7 offered the opportunity for a different path, but Israel chose the path of revenge, which quickly turned to genocide. The state of Israel has failed to care for its own people, it fails to manage its own population with decency, respect, and compassion, and it is now consumed by blood lust for which there is no human solution, only a future of payback, retribution and death. The future of Israel will not be peace, but fire, it will not be hope, but despair, and instead of flowers and vines and fruit, there will be brambles, weeds, and barrenness.

It doesn't matter how many bombs and missiles they receive from Washington, and it doesn't matter how many evangelical pastors support it, and it doesn't matter how many prayers go to the heavens, the road to the next fall of Jerusalem is set. Jerusalem seems destined, not to be the host of a returned Christ, or the scene of the Rapture, but another bloodbath. I am surprised the soil in Israel is not like the red soil of the Australia outback, after so much blood has soaked into it, all that killing in the name of God.

The big fall of Jerusalem was in 587 B.C. That was the decisive fall, God's genocide against his own people. Jerusalem fell in A.D. 70, a few decades after the life of Jesus, and then a century later, and then again under the crusades, and it will fall again.

The people of Israel have forgotten God, they have forgotten the commands of God, and they have forgotten the covenant that God signed with Abram that he would be the father of many peoples, so significant it was that his name changed from Abram to Abraham, the father of many peoples.

Many of the people covered in this covenant lay

dead buried under ruins, many of these people lay dismembered and broken in burnt-out buildings, their bodies rotting in the sun, and many of these people lay dying, while Christians stand over the corpses, hold their New Testament and praying for the victory of the state of Israel, no matter the cost.

It is a mystery to me. My book, Does God Stand with Israel tried to understand the spiritual blindness of Christians about war, how eager they are to support it, how keen they are to pray for it, and how blind they are to the victims of conflict.

Many Christian journalists, academics, pastors, leaders, and public figures are apologists for genocide. They actively lie about what is happening around the world, they actively deceive their listeners, and they are keenly cavalier with the truth, which they curate. They are not innocent bystanders, but proactive participants in the advocacy, defense, and prosecution of genocide in Gaza, and around the world, for they are surrogates of the state.

There is no discernible difference between the church in the American empire and the church in the British empire. This means there is little hope for peace, since the ones who claim to follow the Prince of Peace, love war, they love their empire, and they love killing.

For many Christians in America, the State of Israel must be given a green light to do what it wants because the state of Israel must exist before the Rapture which is the sudden divine gathering of all Christians into heaven. They long for the Rapture, because they don't want to suffer what they believe is the so-called 'Tribulation Period,' a tough time, apparently which precedes the return of Jesus. Then Jesus will be President in Jerusalem for a thousand years. It sounds ridiculous because it is.

Many Christians will happily debate the fine points in this complicated schedule of divine action while children are being murdered in front of them, they simply don't care, they have no compassion. All that matters is this divine timeline, this schedule for the end of the world, the calendar for the so-called 'Last Days.'

What they don't understand, refuse to believe, and oppose, is that the Rapture, the 'Tribulation Period,' the return of the state of Israel, none of it is in the New Testament. It is a fairytale, to which only a fool would subscribe. There are lots of fools today.

Why is there war in the Middle East? Because America wants it, and Israel is their puppet. This is just the continuation of the war since 9/11, the War on Terror, repackaged for a new, gullible, obedient, generation.

The same people in media and government, the same bomb makers, who promoted the War on Terror are promoting this war and the war in Ukraine, as long as bombs are made, as long as profits go up, as long as dividends flow. Gone is Bin Laden, they knew he was in Pakistan but sent Iraq back to the Stone Age anyway. They were in Afghanistan for twenty years. They also destroyed Syria and Libya. Trump continued these wars, and he betrayed the Kurds, and he also supported the genocide in Yemen, so he is not a pacifist, and he will not bring the war in Ukraine to an end with a phone call to his two 'friends' in Ukraine and Russia.

Most American Christians have been bought off, paid off, and bribed. They don't care what is happening in the Middle East. They had their price tag, just look at the lives of most of the Protestant mega church pastors. They have their tax exemptions, their money, their schools, their investments, their properties, and they are laughing all the way to the bank.

After all, how many have stood up to the lies from Donald Trump about migrants eating dogs and cats? How many Christian leaders have called him out on his fascist rhetoric of 'poisoning the blood,' and other rhetoric copied from Adolf Hitler and the Nazi Party? Not many. Not enough. Yes, he is a fascist. He is not Hitler. Hitler is dead. But Trump is still a fascist and with him, you get what you pay for.

Recently another Christian leader has been stood down amid allegations of improper behavior and how the vultures have gathered, to pick what's left of this man, his family, and the lady involved and her family. They call it spiritual adultery. Well, they all vote for Trump, despite all his personal failings, which they regularly excuse, after all, for millions of Christians, Trump is their Messiah.

Spiritual adultery is not having sex in your mind, it is betraying God and replacing God with America, and how many are guilty of this? Spiritual adultery is loving money and pretending to advance the kingdom of God, one million dollars at a time. Spiritual adultery is enabling spiritual abuse through the protection of gossips, slanderers, haters, the envious, the proud, and the bigots. Spiritual adultery is diminishing others made in the image of God because they come from a different nation or have a different skin color. Spiritual adultery is pretending to follow Jesus but only doing it at church on Sunday.

Spiritual adultery is to support war and genocide even though claiming to follow the Prince of Peace. How are they fit for heaven if they ignore such great suffering? How are they fit disciples of Christ if they have no love for others, for children, for the women? How are they fit for heaven, if they have failed in the most basic commandments of holy scripture to love others as Christ has loved them? How are they fit heaven if they have hatred in their hearts for others made in the image of God? How are they fit for heaven if they see the genocide, see the wars, and see the suffering, and then blame the victims of war? How are they fit for heaven if they kill others made in the image of God?

They are not fit for heaven, they know nothing of God, they have forfeited their faith and fallen from grace, and while they rant and rave about abortion, they support war, they support genocide, and they support mass murder.

As these people even Christians? No. Most are not. Jesus said, by their fruit they shall be known. What fruit have these millions of Christians who support Israel, produced?

Ah yes, they go to church, so what, so does the Devil. Ah, yes, they believe in God and Jesus, so what, so does the Devil. Ah, yes, they read their Bibles and pray, so what as it makes little difference in their lives? Ah, yes, they stand for Christian values, so what, do they hear the cries of thousands who are dying from Sudan to Yemen, to Gaza, to Ukraine, to Lebanon?

They don't hear the screams of the kids; they are too busy praising Jesus. They don't hear the cries of the widows; they are too busy listening to the sermon. They don't hear the despair of the innocents; they are too busy doing 'God's work.' Will they stand for Peace? Will they stand for the Prince of Peace? Will they stand for a world of peace? Of course not, peace for them is an American empire, powerful and strong, with bombs and missiles and soldiers and armies. Good for them, another empire to add to the collection of diabolos. He has a great collection now, all the empires of dust, with their false promises, their fake religion, and their dead Christianity.

4.

WHY IS THERE WAR IN THE MIDDLE EAST?

These days, we are at war with Russia, preparing for war with China. America, Britain, and Australia are all, unequivocally and officially on the side of Israel in the Gaza conflict, and the expanding war with Lebanon and Iran. Media commentary and news is biased towards Israel, despite the protests which governments are trying to curtail, minimize, and ban. Any criticism or questioning of any aspect of this unequivocal support of Israel is equated with Anti-Semitism.

Israel's war in the Middle East is the sequel to the War on Terror, and Ukraine's war against Russia is the sequel to the Cold War. Ukraine cannot do anything without the blessing, permission, and support of NATO and Washington. For very strategic decision of the war, Kyiv must get the approval of its Western partners, backers, and suppliers, in other words, the nations who are orchestrating Kyiv's war. In the same way, Israel will do nothing unless given the green light from the White House. Both nations walk a fine line, trying to break free of their colonial masters, but freedom at the end of a leash is not freedom. In both cases, these small states are puppet regimes of America's imperial ambitions. These wars are an extension of the American imperialist state. The apologists for Israel like to call any group opposed to Israel a proxy for Iran, but the reality is that Israel and Ukraine are proxies for America. Ukraine has been America's puppet since 2014 when America helped stage a coup to overthrow the democratically elected government in Kyiv. Israel has been a puppet of America for decades.

Many Christians stand with Ukraine, Israel, and Taiwan, in what some are now daring to call the 'Axis of Evil.' Some of the most avid architects of this unimaginative slogan in government and military circles are themselves unindicted war criminals, famous for their involvement, advocacy, and support of past wars especially the War on Terror, which was a complete failure, but killed millions of innocent people and destroyed four nations, looking for a man they knew was living in Pakistan.

For these apologists, morality is only morality if it is serving the national interest. If the national interest dovetails with morality, then this is the only approved narrative that can be openly admitted. If the national interest is protecting oil fields, then it doesn't matter if Israel commits genocide, for these deaths are of no importance to the national interest, and therefore not worthy of mention. They will be dismissed as irrelevant. If a plane carrying Americans and Europeans is shot down accidentally by a nation at war with America, then it is an act of terror, but if the plane is shot down by a friend of America, it will be described as an unfortunate accident.

There is a vacuous, amoral character to the formation, implementation and defense of state, and this reflects longstanding realist assumptions about the world. What matters to the state and those who defend it, is the national interest. This fine print is never conveyed to the hundreds of pitiful individuals who parrot government talking points more enthusiastically than communists under Stalin.

The amoral character of the state presents a legitimate critique for civil society in a liberal democracy. It is an opportunity for them to openly highlight the inconsistencies, the amoral character of state, the problems with foreign policy. In a democracy, this critical public opinion is at the heart of an open society, even though the state most resolutely has no morality and never will.

The tragedy today is that the sphere of open debate in civil society is closing rapidly and is being replaced by a club of people who imbibe the amoral qualities of the state and accept a worldview of simplistic absolutes, much like children in a way. Perhaps civil society reflects the human mind, and we are now, in the West, in an advanced state of cognitive decline, retreating to the goodies and baddies of childhood, the cops and robbers of TV shows and the bland right and wrong values of Hollywood action films that all end the same way with a fight when the goodie kills the baddie and kisses the girl before the credits roll. Instead of mature, pragmatic, debate, reflection, and critique, we have ideology, propaganda, and sectarianism, and in our minds, we have returned not to the trees and the apes, but to the sandpit, temper tantrums, and childish reasoning about the world in which we live.

The real world isn't like a sandpit, an echo chamber or a playground, but we don't live in the real world, and we don't want to. Gaza has been levelled. Genocide has occurred. Sudan, Yemen, and Ethiopia are at war. Few in the West care. Israel is bombing Lebanon and turned Gaza back to the Stone Age. Yet, educated middle class journalists and political leaders agree that the killing of one Hezbollah leader was worth the deaths of hundreds of civilians. Some are even saying that because these civilians didn't rise up and overthrow Hezbollah, then they deserved to die.

I have read of Christian priests, pastors, ministers and evangelists calling for the death of Hamas, the extermination of Hezbollah and the overthrow of Iran.

Have they forgotten the teachings of Christ, to show love to our enemies, to be peacemakers, to point people to the prince of peace, Jesus? They have all outed themselves, for they don't follow the Savior of the world. The message they preach is one of hate, it is one of revenge, and it is one of payback. None of it is Christian thinking, rhetoric, or belief. More and more Christian leaders are laying aside the gospel to sign on the dotted line to the new gospel of hate. They preach it from their pulpits that somehow Israel's state is sinless, advances the glory of God, and that God approves of sin if it fits their apocalyptic scenario for the end of the world.

More Christian leaders are standing up and standing for war, opposing negotiation, and resisting any ceasefire. They are confident in their theology, sure in their statements, and rest secure in their assumptions about the nature of evil in the world. They know what evil is, but do not condemn it, they stay silent and their views and opinions sound very much like the amoral instruments and agencies of the state, which now owns their voice, their pulpits and their souls.

This is an appropriate time to consider the true nature of evil and sin, not from the point of view of media corporations and the state, but from the viewpoint of the Bible. Is America's support of Israel's war a sin? From the point of view of millions of Americans, war is not a sin if it abides by American values, American nationalism, and American ambitions.

For many in the West, America is righteous, and anyone who stands unquestioningly with America is on the side of truth. This is a moral quagmire. For many, faith and flag have been so mixed up in recent years that millions cannot tell the difference.

I read of an American state that wished to place the Bible in every school, the King James Bible, an out of date and unreadable translation. Each Bible needed to contain the American Constitution and the Bill of Rights. Such arrogant presumption and impudence that the divinely inspired word of God should share the same pages as the fallible scribblings of uninspired men.

With the passing of the anniversary of the October 7 incursion and mass kidnapping, much has been said by political leaders in Australia past and present about good and evil, and how confident they are, that their definition is the correct one, and that they have both the authority and the right to determine the geography of evil. I don't take my understanding of the nature of sin, the nature of evil, and the nature of wickedness from politicians, but from the Bible, which I believe is inspired by the Holy Spirit. Why do so many Christians place their faith in people, and not in God?

5.

DOES GOD BLESS SIN?

St Paul asked his readers in his letter to the Romans whether God blesses sin, and whilst it is such a strange question to ask, it is easy to see it playing out in our world today, in the awful destruction of the people of Gaza to fulfil, in the minds of some, that it is God's intent for some of his elect to suffer destruction for the betterment of others whom he loves. Paul asks his readers,

> 'What shall we say then? Shall we continue in sin, that grace may abound? God forbid. How shall we, that are dead to sin, live any longer therein?' (Romans 6: 1-2).

The perverse rhetoric from many Christian leaders to 'destroy Hamas' and 'kill Hezbollah,' and 'defend Israel,' are examples of rhetoric that have no place in the Christian community, are not Christian and are not examples of Christlike speech. Advocating for the murder of anyone, regardless of their political affiliation is rhetoric that one might find from centuries of church states and the evil wickedness of the day when the church wielded the sword but is out of place in the day of secular governments, democratic politics, the rule of law, and professional armies.

But this perversion of the teaching of Christ is not surprising. Capitalism, and the intimate relationship between capitalism and war, has profoundly changed the moral codes of Christians so that what the New Testament saw as a set of sins, is now embraced as virtues. Church is essential to minimize the damage Christians can inflict on the social and economic order. Christianity, as a ritual not a life means that the social and political order transforms the moral character of Christians more decisively that Jesus.

Recently, I have been thinking about sin. It has occurred to me that while the Bible talks about sin, it rarely defines sin in the way we would like it to be defined, and thus, consequently we ought to exercise caution when we speak of it. The Bible speaks of the idea of 'missing the mark' an image from archery, of missing the bullseye (Romans 3: 23). The Bible speaks of sin as a transgression (1 John 3: 4), which is a misstep, or it employs the idea of stumbling (James 3:2). The Bible also speaks of sin as principle of power within the heart of a person (Romans 6: 23). This is just a simple introduction.

The Bible is also very clear about what sin is not. It is not diabolos who forces us to sin. He is not responsible for our decisions. Whilst he can tempt us, he cannot control us, and even though he is the prince of this world and has blinded the world to the things of God (2 Corinthians 4:4), it doesn't mean we are without personal responsibility. The obsession with Satan in some corners of the Christian community is good for diabolos. It is without any evidence from the

New Testament. We sin. We are responsible beings. We are moral beings. Our sin falls on us. We are accountable. We are to blame, no one else (Ezekiel 18: 1-32). The Bible clearly, consistently, and comprehensively rejects a hierarchy of sin and repudiates the moralism of our age (James 2: 10-20; Romans 3: 23). At the same time, we are not responsible for the sin of others. That is on them. Accepting personal responsibility is at the heart of the Christian faith.

Whilst the Bible employs various images and ideas, we grapple with the specifics, as well as the nature of sin. Is it because we are sinful people? Is it because we don't care about sin? Is it because how we understand sin has changed? What were the factors or causes which led to our changing perception of sin.

The question that I pose is about capitalism, which is a word we often use to describe our economic and political world. Whilst it is fraught with problems, it is nonetheless a kind of shorthand. Some call it the 'industrial system,' or others, the 'market-based society,' but all of them are trying to say the same thing, that what we have is a system, or a structure that shapes, orders, and influences not only the economy and social life, but our very beings. Thus, the impact of capitalism is not superficial. It goes to the heart of our humanity. Capitalism changed us.

The myth of AI is that our belief in the 'ever-present unchanging human character,' will be transformed. Critics call it the 'transhuman agenda,' but it is largely a myth, a fiction, a wordplay. Humanity has evolved and changed over the years. Diet, the eradication of disease, and medicinal advances have changed the human body. In a little town south of the city of Sendai in Japan, Shiroishi, is a rebuilt replica castle, made largely of wood, according to the original design, and for most tourists, both Japanese and non-Japanese, it feels a bit small, a bit cramped, and claustrophobic. The reason is that Japanese people in the sixteenth century were smaller people, by and large, by virtue of a diet without much meat. Many of the famous 'samurai' of the past, were small men by our average height today. When you visit reconstructed ferro-concrete castles in Japan, they have always made sure the space fits the modern Japanese person, so few people bump their heads around every corner.

It is not only diet, but technology. More recently, we have pacemakers and implants, artificial limbs and prosthetics, the growth in industrial medicines and pharmaceuticals and so on. These are changes because of technology and science. We have changed, but we do not recognize the change. This is probably because it has been subtle and gradual over time.

These physical and technological changes are profound, and they are influenced by many factors including wealth. In other words, wealthier people are more likely to take advantage of many of the benefits of technology that may improve our lifestyle and longevity. To facilitate a fairer distribution of the benefits of these technological changes is one of the reasons for the welfare state. Our society has also changed us, and this goes to how our social, economic and political fabric is woven, organized, and promoted.

In feudalism, the method of the state was to keep people in misery, poverty, disease, and death, so they would not rebel. In capitalism, it is different. Capitalism is about the effective and productive use of human resources and so the state ideally needs a fit population. The heart of capitalism is the division of labour to produce commodities to be sold in the market. Once a nation moves from a transition period to full-blown industrial change, this has and will transform the whole society.

A lot can be said about the difference between feudalism and capitalism. In capitalism, the goal is wealth creation, as it was in the intermediary phase, mercantilism, which comes from our word 'mercantile' which means 'trade.' This too, had a goal of wealth creation, but like feudalism, most of the wealth stayed at the top, and while there was a reorganization of power in the state, it did not change the life of the ordinary person.

In feudalism, the goal was stability, and the absence of change, the acceptance of one's lot in life, the repudiation of individual initiative, and everyone knew their place. Shows like Downton Abbey and Upstairs Downstairs are examples of feudal values, and demonstrate that even though capitalism came to Britain, it brought with it much of the repugnant filth of feudalism, including stringent class pretensions which are largely incompatible with an industrial system.

The American Civil War was the same. Slavery was incompatible with the values of an industrial state. Slavery in the South for agriculture, propped up by the vile Calvinist doctrine of election applied to slavery was indicative of a set of feudal values that had no place in an emerging capitalist, industrial system. The Civil War was not a battle between the states and the federal government, but it was a battle between feudal and capitalist values.

It is impossible to run a capitalist system with feudal values. Capitalism is about dynamism, growth, and wealth creation. Had the South won, there would be no America today. As for making American great again, this ideology echoes the Civil War rhetoric, as the enemy is presented as the federal government in Washington. The 'deep state,' is just a new version of the Mason Dixon line, without the reference to slaves or the Lost Cause, but MAGA is a Lost Cause.

The irony is that Trump's MAGA is a recipe for turning the middle class into the poor white trash of North America. American capitalism, to survive, needs millions of immigrants, the more the merrier, to work the factories which Trump wants to return home. Capitalist societies need millions of people to work the dirty, difficult, and dangerous jobs in return for generational economic security. Otherwise, the cost of production will rise, cost of living will rise, and so will inflation. Closing borders to foreign goods will do the same. It will not make America stronger economically. MAGA is a recipe for pre-Civil War values, a recipe for poverty. If MAGA is allowed to proceed in America, the future will be state-based price controls to force down the cost of living for the millions of Americans who want smaller government. If adopted, the economic chaos of MAGA policies will necessitate Roosevelt-style social and economic controls on the American economy.

What does this mean in terms of sin? How are Christians to respond to capitalism? Well, Christians have already responded to capitalism. These changes took place at the end of the nineteenth century and early twentieth century. A new phase began in the postwar era, a new response shaped by the Cold War. Since 9/11 we are in a new phase. There have been three or four distinct episodes. We have been living with around 150 years of Christian interaction with capitalism. It is a period of intense propaganda, curtailment of religious power, and conscious spiritual manipulation of doctrines, ideas, and beliefs, not as vicious as communism or fascism, but just as pervasive, just as wide-ranging, and just as effective. Propaganda with a smile, a bucket of cash and a warm handshake is still propaganda.

The first thing to say is that following Jesus repudiates the essence of all human institutions because it is from God. God overturns, God overthrows, God unsettles. True Christianity is calling people back to God, and whatever human institution exists, this call to faith is incompatible with that institution.

What this means is that the Christianity of the New Testament is incompatible with capitalism. It also means that Christianity was incompatible with feudalism, and it was also incompatible with the Roman Empire which preceded the rise of feudalism. In every age, the one who follows Jesus is at odds with the social, political, and economic order.

The second thing to say is that in capitalism, Christians have redefined sin, and changed the way they believe God views sin, and they have changed the way they are to engage in an understanding of sin. For Christians who believe in God, follow Jesus, and wish to apply the New Testament in their life, they will encounter this social compromise, and they will either capitulate or fight against it. As in feudalism, so in capitalism, most of the seeds of faith will be strangled by the weeds, the thorns, and the brambles of our society. Yes, many will go to church on Sunday, but they are not followers of Jesus.

What does this mean? Well, capitalist Christians have redefined sin because it doesn't fit with our capitalist world. It doesn't suit our lifestyle. It doesn't abide with our expectations and desires. Capitalism has profoundly changed the way we view sin, and this is a problem because capitalism has blinded us to the nature of sin, the power of sin, and the reality of sin.

The third thing to say is that because of this tension between what God wants and our society demands, there are profound, inexplicable contradictions. Church is essential in capitalism to minimize the damage Christians can do to society. Their faith is expressed entirely in church on Sunday and then the rest of the week they are back in the capitalist system.

Capitalism demands complete obedience and so we hear of Christians openly supporting war, relishing the destruction of nations, people, and children. Yet it is all inconsistent with a Christian faith. They hold to two opposing ideologies at the same time, or it appears to be the case. The reality is, tragically, that their heart faith is not following Jesus. They follow Christ only at church. Indeed, they redefine the life of faith to be exclusively walked on the road, path, or highway to church on Sunday, and the rest of the week they are loyal to capitalism, loyal to the state, and loyal to the world.

This hatred of others is welcomed, encouraged, and enticed by the church, especially in North America, enveloping a new sectarianism within religion, along political lines. Christians who so eagerly, regularly, enthusiastically embrace war as the answer to all problems, are not followers of Jesus. In their heart is hate, pure and simple, and God does not abide hatred, as all hatred was absorbed in the body of Christ on the cross, so humans who reinvent hate, who harbor hate, and who relish hate, stand alone, and are not with God.

We must remember, that in capitalism, what medieval Christianity saw as wickedness, is embraced today by Christians as virtue. The way morality was weighed by the church transformed participation in the capitalist system required modification, amendment, and adjustments to a set of principles incompatible with the market.

The Christian church today believes, generally, that lust is synonymous with sex and sexual identity. Trump is exempt of course, from this and as part of the MAGA movement, Trump stands for family values, even though he has had several families.

The Bible rejects moralism and teaches instead a broad and comprehensive view of sin, how it has to do with our heart, and we stand as imperfect beings before a perfect and holy God (Jeremiah 17: 9, Matthew 15: 19). Both feudalism and capitalism are unable to interpret the heart, it is the prerogative, the territory, and the sphere of the divine, and so both systems define sin as an external action rather than a heartfelt attitude.

In capitalism, all the seven deadly sins bar one, are virtues in the church. For those who are unfamiliar with these medieval sins, they are greed, pride, wrath, lust, gluttony, sloth, and envy. In feudalism, the church held nations back, kept people in poverty, exploited class divisions to advance their power, and used the state to kill its enemies. In capitalism, the social contract between the state and church is simple: tax exemptions in return for a theology compatible with greed. Every church has their own spin on these seven deadly sins.

Many Christians in America today and around the world eagerly embrace most of the seven deadly sins as part of their compromise with the values of a capitalist society. The exception is sex, which is seen as lust. Christians can be greedy, angry, envious, prideful, gluttonous, and slothful and can enjoy the kingdom of God, the applause of their friends, and the approval of God. This is the compromise with the capitalist system, and it reflects obedience, loyalty, and capitulation. The state can rest easy because it knows that Christians are no threat to the state because they are willing participants in the spiritual contract underpinning the social order.

What this means is that as a result of this compromise, Jesus is of no importance to their life, and they will go to war, they will kill others made in God's image, and they will grieve the Spirit of God, but they don't care, because all that matters is what they can get for themselves in this social and economic order. The Bible teaches that our hearts are the problem, not our actions, because our actions come from our inner beings. Our hearts need spiritual change, and it is only God who can heal us (Ezekiel 36: 26, 2 Corinthians 5: 17).

A Christian who understands that faith is about a heart transformed will not care about rules, regulations, and rituals, or the stench of public morality, and they will, inevitably resist political tyranny because of their steadfast belief in the profligate, overflowing, and enduring grace and mercy of a loving God. For a Christians, 'Christ is Lord,' is their political manifesto, it is their rejection of public morality, and it is their embrace of a God for all of their life, not for show, not for Sunday, and not for others, a life embracing the kingdom of God.

A Christian who reads the Bible and sincerely desires to follow Christ is on a dangerous path for they are rebelling against the social and economic order, and whilst they may go to heaven, the strongest opposition they will face will be from the church, which has made its pact with the world, and all its evils.

6.

IS ISRAEL
AN APARTHEID STATE?

When was the last time you went to a zoo? When I lived in Japan, I would often visit castles, extant and authentic, ruined, and reconstructed. The best ones are high in the mountains, their stones covered in moss, trees for their turrets and the forest for their domain. One of the postwar ferro-concrete castles is in the town of Odawara, near Tokyo. It was a famous town significant in Japanese history, but now it is just another stop on the Tokaido Shinkansen. In front of the castle, near a delightful park which was full of the postwar hybrid cherry blossom trees, was a concrete slab which housed a family of rather unhappy and gaunt looking monkeys in a rusted cage, and an equally disheartened, sickly, and sad elephant. Why someone thought that monkeys and an elephant were needed to sit in front of a ferroconcrete castle is a mystery to me. Soon afterwards, I went to Ueno Zoo which was more like a prison, and animals from all over the world lived on various slabs of concrete, with a little bit of dirt, maybe some grass if they were lucky. The smell of manure was everywhere.

Now, whilst the manure was pungent, it would be overpowered by the foul stench of the Western orientalists, that cabal of cultural apologists, (usually tenured academics), who will defend everything Japanese as being pure, unique, wonderful, and indicative of a great culture. No doubt, some would argue that in Japan, they pour concrete in a special way reflecting ancient tradition, that the rusted cage reflected the philosophy of Zen Buddhism, that Japanese monkeys digest food differently. They would argue that any criticism of Ueno Zoo reflected cultural imperialism.

I could see the sickly monkeys with my own eyes, and the emaciated elephant, and the poor kangaroos crouched in Ueno Zoo with no room to move. I know abuse when I see it and so do the apologists, but their job is to lie about Japan, and lie they do. These apologists have lied about Japan their entire careers. If they tell the truth, they will lose their jobs and their free trips to Japan paid for by the Japanese government. They would lose the respect of the corrupt Japanese state who cares less for their own people than they do for the monkeys in cages.

Why am I talking about cages and zoos, and monkeys and elephants? It is simple. The Palestinians are living in a human zoo, in cages, in the Gaza Strip and the West Bank. They are treated like animals, live in poverty, denied human rights, denied respect and human dignity. This prison has been in Israel for decades. While young Israelis danced in the desert, just over the fence in Gaza, the Palestinians lived in their prison, in brokenness, hopelessness, and despair. If there was no October 7, no one would care, no one would notice, and no one would pay attention to the worst human rights crisis in the world since Apartheid in South Africa.

The state of mind of the Palestinian people, their conditions, their humanity is dictated by a quasi-religious state which has decreed that the Palestinians have no human integrity or dignity. This corrupt failed state is a rogue state, and even though it is run by Washington, it is out of control, wanting to plunge the whole region into war.

Just as in Japan, there is a huge cabal of Western apologists in government, media, the church, and civil society who don't want us to know the truth about the Palestinians, who don't care about the truth, and who know they are engaged in orchestrated deceit. Israel is a failed state. It is not a state where God is honored. It is a state which has no future beyond the American shield.

How are we to describe this mess? Some use the term, the 'open air prison,' and others a 'zoo,' and yet others call this system, an 'Apartheid System.' They are all synonyms really, for they all describe the same thing. That is exactly what it is. The fact that thousands of Christian pastors in the West support the state of Israel, ignore the suffering of the Palestinian people, and lie about the New Testament tells me that these men and women are not Christians, they have departed from God, they have forsaken their faith, and their continued existence is a middle finger to the divine. It is the action of these people and thousands like them that have disgraced the good news of Jesus

Christ and made Christianity repugnant to the people of the Middle East. God will not forget their apostasy. I have written extensively about the errors of Christian Zionism in an earlier book, *'Does God Stand with Israel? A Christian Response to Gaza,'* published by *Hidden Road Publishing,* 2024.

Israel is a failed state, a rogue state, a broken state. Some fortunate few in Israel are citizens, while the rest are treated like dogs. It is a sick and twisted society when this is tolerated. They claim legitimacy as a civilized society. They are anything but civilized. People living behind a fence are not free.

But no nation in Europe or in the New World is without blood on their hands. The only difference is that other nations have tried to build just and fair societies. Israel has not. They don't care. They have lived on the coattails of the American empire for long enough and it is time to grow up. It is time to make the hard choices. It is time for people to be free. If they want help, they are dozens of models, for all of Europe has been there, and all the West, and most of the East can show the way. Israel today, however, is on the wrong path, they know it, we know it, and God knows it. It is a dead end and will lead to ruin.

But there is another critique. This is the idea that the state of Israel is illegitimate, that it is a white settler colonial project when the land was stolen and continues to be stolen, and that the land is unceded by the Palestinians. This broader critique is often extended to all the other white settler colonies such as Australia and America. They say that they too are illegitimate states, which stole the land, that the land is unceded indigenous land. There are lots of slogans like this, 'always has been, always will be indigenous land.'

I don't support the 'stolen state,' 'stolen land' hypothesis. It is true, Gaza and the West Bank are open air prisons, they are like zoos for animals, they live in an apartheid state, and this is all true. But I believe that just as Spain overcame Franco, and Chile, Pinochet, and Germany Hitler, and Australia, the White Australia Policy, and America, segregation, Israel too, can join other nations through a difficult but essential path, to peace, reconstruction, reconciliation and a genuine, open society. A truly equitable, free and open Israel is not impossible.

Just as many in Israel don't want peace with Palestine, many Palestinians don't want peace either. There is an industry of 'human rights' workers, and activists in the West. They all have good jobs they are all wealthy and part of the Palestinian elite. They all seem to escape the war and conflict, and they all have strong opinions. They also have their agenda which they are careful not to share.

This Palestinian cabal doesn't want peace because if Israel follows Spain and Germany and America and creates a new nation where all are equal under the law, these activists will be out of a job, no one will interview them and no one will remember their names or read their books. These activists support the 'stolen state' hypothesis. They don't want peace. They want war, but they will not fight in this war. After all, many live in New York, drinking cocktails, attending conferences, and wearing designer clothes, while Gaza burns.

The 'stolen state' argument doesn't come from America, but from Europe, the Old World. The Old World hates the New, because new states are the future. The Old World is dying. The Europeans powers raped the world for centuries, their empires destroying countless cultures. Now, they are dying out, their birthrates collapsing, their population declining, and they are becoming irrelevant in global affairs. It was out of weakness that Europe banded together to form the European Union. The only source of migration is from the nations they raped in the past. Europe now rejects them because they want to return to their fake Christian heritage, which they paint with rose tinted glasses. That history is soaked in blood, violence and religious conflict, not Christians against Islam but Christians against Christians. They don't want migrants, but their desires to raise the birthrate will end in failure, as I have written in my book, *'Baby Race: Are low national birthrates a blessing or a curse?'* published by Hidden Road Publishing, 2024. I commend this book to anyone who wants to understand the reality, the causes, and the consequences of low birthrates in the West, and we need to start by rejecting the fake news of the Far-Right.

The Europeans lie about history all the time. They are saying that the Ukraine conflict is the first war in Europe since WW2. This is a lie. In the 1990s, Yugoslavia broke up and there was a major war, or several wars. Yugoslavia is in Europe. They forget this of course. It doesn't fit Russophobia and the NATO narrative.

They also forget that in the 1950s and 1960s while Europe was climbing out of the consequences of the war, their colonies in Asia and Africa were breaking free, including violent struggles which Europe opposed. No European power in the West fought for freedom against the Axis Powers because after the war, they wanted all their colonies back, but Malaya, Indonesia, Vietnam, and India, among others, wanted freedom. For over 30 years colonies were in conflict with their colonial masters, eager to be free. Let me repeat so you understand. Europe and Britain and America fought Hitler for land and power, not for democracy and freedom. As soon as the Axis Powers were defeated, Europe and Britain wanted their colonies back and they denied freedom in every single case.

In other words, what happened in Palestine was just another land grab, and a civil war, which the Israelis won. During the tenure of the British, several terrorist organizations run by Jewish patriots caused havoc. These militia formed the basis of what is now the Israeli Defense Force. The terrorist became the soldier, the invader became the citizen, a war was won, and there were victors and the defeated. Israel is a legitimate state because 'to the victor belong the spoils.'

Why stop at 'white settler' colonies? It is such an arbitrary choice. Italy, Germany, France, and other nations are also illegitimate nation states, according to the logic of this 'stolen state' thesis. These Western European nations are all European imperialist projects, and these nations too, need to revert to the original, natural forms of social and political organization. They all stole land from the previous owners and political entities through war and conflict, usurped monarchs, dukes, and fiefs. This means that all nations are illegitimate, and we must return all nations to their previous owners and rulers. Europe, for starters, will cease to exist, and the EU will need to disband.

Military victory in history is a fundamental principle of international relations. Tamper with this and the whole international system will collapse. In this argument are we seeing the revision of European boundaries that predate the formation of European nations at the end of the nineteenth century? Of course not, but why not? These nationalist movements in Europe were also, according to the 'stolen state theory,' just another form of land theft, so all European nation states are also illegitimate. How far do we go back? How many centuries?

Those who support 'stolen state' theories don't want to live in community with others, they want their pure society, a society which they will create in their own image. But this is not society. Society is where all kinds of people live together as equals under the law, one law for all people. Once a state is formed, the morality of the state is the way all people within its boundaries are included in that society. How this is done, how it is measured and how it is achieved, is the standard of how we judge that society. The reality is that most states mess it up and have not worked it out. Some states have done better than others. Other states were designed by colonial powers simply as lines on a map, and so will take generations to work out their problems.

In the case of Israel, the treatment of Palestinians has been a disgrace, it has been shameful, and yet everything Israel does is protected by the cabal of Western apologists who will not allow even scrutiny of any aspect of the Israeli Project.

There was no 'invasion' on October 7, but a prison breakout. It is the same land, marked by the fence, the prison fence, the steel cage. The media lies constantly about this. Gaza is Israel's human zoo. Gaza is a huge prison for millions of people who are deemed unworthy of human dignity. On October 7, some of the inmates got out of the prison. We can live in the fantasy of unhinged reality that it was an 'unprovoked attack,' or we can take steps towards a genuinely humane society. Don't bet on it. The future is just more blood, more killing, and more revenge. Don't forget, very few people in the West want Israel to succeed. The last thing they want is real peace, real reconciliation, and a real society. The West wants Israel to fail.

In the same way, October 7 was not an 'unprovoked' event. It was a breakout by a people living in a prison. Everything in the Gaza Strip is a creation of the Israeli state. Tragically, many of my Christian brothers and sisters are apologists for Israeli genocide, they are spiritually unhinged, they do not have an ounce of compassion. For them, their patriotism blinds them, their prejudice binds them, and their ignorance confuses them. They all hide behind the American shield. For them, this is just another war on the road to the return of Jesus, and they don't care, because they believe the Jews are God's chosen people, in other words, he unconditionally, and exclusively loves the people of the state of Israel, even though this is taught nowhere in the Bible. If American Christianity today is the highpoint of spirituality, then God help us, for what a disgrace it is, to see Christian people who claim to follow Jesus, call for the death of Hamas, Hezbollah or Iran, instead of calling for peace, living for peace, and dying for peace, following the Prince of Peace, whom they have forgotten.

What is the way forward for Israel and its apartheid state? Is it killing their enemies until they are all dead? This is the strategy promoted by Christian Zionists, and many apologists for genocide in the West, an endless struggle against the enemies of Israel until all are vanquished. This is the strategy of the Trump White House and many American conservatives. They insist on the loyalty test, that everyone must condemn Hamas, support the genocide in Gaza, or at least pretend that it is not happening, and support the wider war against Lebanon and Iran. This is the colonial puppet view of American foreign policy, Israel will continue America's War on Terror against Gaza, Lebanon and Iran with American bombs and Israeli troops. Israel will take the lead until it becomes such a quagmire that Congress will call for American 'boots on the ground,' or support for 'voluntary militia groups' like those operating now inside Russia and Ukraine.

The 'war of conquest' model is also the strategy of the current administration in Israel, bringing to mind 1 Samuel of all places to justify the killing of thousands of children and equating the people of Palestine with the people of Amalek, from the ancient past. Surely, Netanyahu knows his Hebrew Bible, that Saul disobeyed Samuel, and this led to his demise. Does he not remember that due to its apostasy, Jerusalem itself was burned to the ground by God in 586 B.C. Does he not remember that there were no Jews in the ancient near East, only Israelites, and that the 'Jew' really comes from the days of Jeremiah the prophet and the return of the survivors of war to the land promised generations later. That is the beginning of Judaism and Jewish identity, not the ancient past of Abraham, the days of Moses, or the monarchy.

There are other alternatives to Netanyahu's 'scorched earth policy,' and one does not need to look very far for it. The one supported by the American ruling class is the 'two state solution.' It is also the preferred European approach to the settlement of the

'Palestinian Question,' and it is also the preferred choice for the thousands of wealthy Palestinians in exile, who hate Israel as much as Israel hates them. This would invariably be a UN solution, with 'boots on the ground,' and a permanent European and American presence in Israel, at least for the foreseeable future.

It is a bold plan, the Two State Solution. There is plenty of time to run this model somewhere else to see if it works. We could start with America, after all, using the same logic for the 'two state solution,' America stole the land of the First Nations Peoples, so America could adopt a 'two state solution.' Maybe Spain could do the same for the Basque peoples, and maybe Australia could do the same for the Indigenous people.

The reality is that the 'two state solution' would never be applied anywhere except Israel and we need to ask the question, why is that? Why is Israel not allowed to have its own territorial integrity, but Ukraine is? Why does America insist on total victory against Russia and yet promotes a 'two state solution' for Israel? It is an inconsistent foreign policy.

There could be peace tomorrow in Ukraine if America allows the two dissident republics some form of tentative autonomy, with a referendum in ten years, local governance, with obligations to both Russia and Kyiv, the end of hostilities and the path forward for reconstruction and peace. It could happen tomorrow, but no, America will not allow two rural republics to enjoy any form of autonomy unless they support American control of Ukraine, the presence of NATO, American bases and missiles pointed at Russia.

There is a third model which no one seems to want to talk about because they prefer either endless war or constant conflict. Anyone can destroy. Anyone can tear down. Anyone can discourage. That is easy. It is difficult to build, it is difficult to create, and it is difficult to lead. But Israel must, and they must give the middle finger to the Christian Zionists and their fairy tale theology, fake compassion, and false piety. They need to break free of the American colonial yoke which binds them these days, as well as the echo chambers of Zionist lobbies in the West, and Israel needs peace with Palestine, permanently.

This third option is to create one state, open to all people, under one law, one legal system, one set of rights and freedoms, and one citizenship. In other words, Israel should create a nation-state where Palestinian and Jew live together in the same house, with the same rights of land ownership. This includes the bringing in of Israel's enemies into the state of Israel. This is the idea that the Palestinians are brought into Israel and made equal participants in that nation-state, equal under the law, and equal in terms of social and economic enfranchisement, the end of the apartheid, the end of conflict, and the end of the 'two state' fairytale.

It has happened before. Nelson Mandela was a terrorist and went to prison for it, but he ended up as President of South Africa. Sinn Fein was associated with the Irish Republican Army (IRA) but over many years, Sinn Fein was brought into the state, electoral success and today is the largest political party in the Northern Ireland Assembly. Yasser Arafat was an Arab nationalist, but many in the West saw him as a terrorist, but his leadership of the Palestinian Liberation Organization (PLO) saw him rise to become the head of the Palestinian Authority.

Israel will not prevail against Iran, and they will

not stay in Lebanon forever, and they will not exterminate Hamas or Hezbollah, for their policies have created another generation of boys and girls who will grow up to hate Israel.

Perhaps that is the strategic goal of Netanyahu, to scuttle any hope for lasting peace for the next fifty years, so that Israel will be constantly at war. The sowing of chaos is an American strategy, and this is perhaps where Netanyahu got the scorched earth policy of enduring hate. Listening to Israeli leaders talking about the future is surreal. Now. Many Israelis are talking about extending new settlements into Gaza, of new beachfront properties, and new infrastructure, but what of the 2 million people of Gaza?

Unless there is a genuine social and political revolution in Israel that decides to bring the nation into the twenty-first century, there is no future there. No one will accept Israeli control, no one will trust anything Israel says again, and for the next generation, Israel will be under prosecution for war crimes, for genocide, and for its neglect of its own people. Aside from Christian Zionists in Australia and America, the world is sick of Israel and its current trajectory away from civilization to a world of payback, blood, and death.

But as soon as America leaves, then Israel will be most certainly destroyed. Israel will go the same way as one of those ill-fated crusader cities in the Middle East in the Middle Ages. Without external support, they were overcome by others, or the desert simply swallowed them up. The so-called 'Kingdom of Jerusalem' lasted only two centuries (1099-1291) and it seems likely the state of Israel will go the same way.

What will happen to the Christian Zionists? They don't care about Israel; they only promote their fairytale theology for money. Look at them, they are all rich. No, when America leaves, they will make up another theology and keep their followers in financial bondage some other way. Given the appalling, hideous, and criminal actions of Israel since October 8, 2023, Israel will have few friends in the West, except perhaps in America and its puppet in Asia, Australia. But that will not be enough because America's support of Israel is not eternal, unconditional and enduring, it is conditional, it is strategic, and one day, will come to an end.

7.

WHY DOES AMERICA
SUPPORT ISRAEL?

America supports Israel today because of oil and it was all an accident of history. Israel is in the right place at the right time. The black liquid that comes from the earth and powers the world, is the reason for the Middle East, its nature, its character, and its significance. Without oil, most people today would have the same ignorance about the Middle East as they do about other parts of the world of no strategic significance to geopolitics.

The Middle East is a central part of the 'oil system' and it is their destiny, for good or ill. The 'oil system,' emerged in the world from the late nineteenth century until the present time, it powered America and Russia, and it accounts for most of the conflicts around the world, which are essential energy wars over natural resources, how to power the economy, and the military. Up until perhaps the Great War, capitalism was driven by coal, and now it is driven by oil.

Israel's existence and the emergence of Saudi Arabia were both due to the end of the Ottoman Empire at the conclusion of the Great War. Both came under the influence of the British Empire. Like many colonies and former properties of dead empires, Saudi Arabia and Israel had a tumultuous and complicated prehistory. Saudi Arabia was formed in 1932 and in 1938 oil was discovered. This changed the balance of power in the region, and in the world. Alongside Russia and America, Saudi Arabia is in the top 3 oil producers on the planet. Oil is the basis of both the Russian and American empires and spheres of influence. Most oil reserves in the world come from the Middle East, and America has ties to most nations with large oil reserves such as Qatar, Iraq, UAE, and Kuwait.

The first Gulf War in the 1990s was to protect American oil interests in Kuwait. The War on Terror justified America's invasion of Iraq, which is now largely under American control. UAE and Qatar are allied to America. Saudi Arabia is allied to America, and when Israel (and America) defeats Iran, Iran too, will come under American control. At least, that is the plan.

Israel exists as a front for the pursuit of American oil wars in the Middle East. Israel is an oil importer and arms importer and is almost entirely dependent on American military support and protection. Whilst Israel's nuclear capacity is shrouded in mystery, it seems that at various stages, France, America, and Britian, among others, had their role to play in aiding and covering up the development of Israel's nuclear arsenal. As a nuclear power, this not only affords Israel protection, but it also ensures American scrutiny and control.

As I said in the beginning. It is all an accident of history. The Bible is silent on all of these developments. It has nothing to say beyond the idea of providence, and it has nothing to do with the fairytale of the Rapture. It is all about oil.

The oil system is incredibly powerful. The oil system has prevented global movements towards reining in climate change. The oil system is behind opposition to research on alternative energy sources. The oil system is behind almost all the Western support for Israel, aside from the apocalytes in the Christian church, but even there, the oil system is behind that as well. The apocalytes are those millions of Christians who are disciples to apocalyptic thinking that only converges on Jerusalem and Israel, where all of God's enemies are the enemies of American foreign policy. These apocalytes did not exist in Christianity before the oil system and will disappear when oil ceases to dominate the global economy.

The American and European war against Chinese electric cars (EVs) is part of the oil war. China can make cheap EVs so that billions of people can drive cheap cars on electricity. This would change the world, but the oil industry is opposed to it. They want Americans to drive cars on gas. That's it. After encouraging the Chinese to build electric vehicles, the West doesn't want them. China has a cheap and reliable way forward out of the world's reliance on carbon, but America, Australia, and the Western nations want oil or expensive EVs made only in America.

There are lots of climate deniers in the Protestant

evangelical wing in America. Behind the spirit of evangelicalism are the national myths of America, and at the heart of this is support for oil-based prosperity. This is not a conspiracy, but rather it is a culture of oil that is tied to much of the American dream, and ideology, that oil comes from the earth and is one of God's gifts to the nation, and this is all connected to the American Project and the American Ideal. Those who question oil, tread on the legacy of this Dream and Ideal, and inherited experience, even though the use of oil is killing the world's environment and destabilizing the Middle East.

Without oil, Russia and America will fall, they will collapse, and a new world will form in its ashes. Nuclear power was a supplement to oil, but its association with war is the reason for ambiguity over its effects and use.

Britian didn't want Israel to become a state. That much is clear from the Mandate for Palestine, and this explains the revolt, the violence, and the civil war, what Palestinians called the Nakba. Britain was good at having an empire, but a failure at letting go, and the mess of Israel mirrors that of India, and Malaya, a time of absolute chaos. Britain bears much responsibility for the problems in the Middle East. America inherits Britain's mess, and what they inherit is effectively a house of cards.

The weakness of Britain at the time was due to the war, and the effective bankruptcy of the British state. Britain never recovered from the Great War, and the empire was a casualty of the Second World War. Behind this imperial collapse was the horror of the Holocaust, which caught the entire world by surprise. There had always been pogroms, persecution of Jewish people, but it was the industrial scale, the planning, the orchestration of genocide that was different. It took decades of planning, hundreds of thousands of people were involved to implement it.

The worst thing about the Holocaust was that millions of middle-class people in a capitalist society, supported it. They were not ignorant, uneducated, poor, diet-starved people. They were not an uncontrolled mob. They were not the 'floating mass,' a term that was used for the Indonesian poor in the 1950s. They were educated, and they saw no problem with the mass extermination of the Jews.

Capitalism was supposed to represent the end of the old regime, the old prejudice, the old values, but it wasn't, and it isn't. We remember Pol Pot, who tried to create a pre-modern society using genocide. We remember Stalin who tried to create a socialist society using genocide. We remember Mao, who tried to create a communist society using genocide. But Germany was a capitalist society, like ours today, and Germany engaged in genocide against the Jewish people of Europe, murdering over 6 million of them. There is no real difference in the economic system between Nazi Germany and any capitalist society today.

Capitalist societies can perpetrate the worst mass murders in history, on an industrial scale, completely supported by most of the educated population. The German people loved their Third Reich. The German people loved their Fuhrer. The German people believed in their Aryan myths and ideologies. The German people saw the Jews and Slavs as animals and less than human. The idea that Germans didn't know about the Holocaust is a lie. They knew. They supported it.

In other words, the idea of Israel, the dream of

Zionism, the expectation of a homeland suddenly became an absolute necessity, and whatever you think of the Nakba, behind it is this frantic, genuine fear, among Jews that they needed a home, and the best home was their ancestral abode.

Behind most of the support for Israel is the oil system, for opposition to Israel will lead to its inevitable demise, and chaos in the Middle East, beyond the intolerable levels that already exist today. America must support Israel, for if it does not, the Arabs will easily destroy Israel as successive elected representatives have engaged in violent pogroms and genocide against the Palestinians and others. If Israel is pressed, it will use nuclear weapons against the Middle East and even one explosion will cause a rupture in the global economy, and the potential end of American power.

The pressures on the American state, the existence of Israel, and the problems in the Middle East are a parable on capitalism. It is an inherently unstable system. It causes unbelievable suffering as well as prosperity. It forces nations to do the unthinkable in terms of morality. The American empire remains entirely dependent on oil and explains its presence in the Middle East. America is an oil power. Russia is an oil power.

What will happen to capitalism when a new energy source is found? It could be fusion, it could be nuclear, it could be something else. When this does happen, the Middle East will be as useful to the world as horses are to roads, it will become as significant to the world as oil lamps on the street corner and it will become as relevant to the world as the fax machine, the printing press, and coal. When this happens, I believe, the state of Israel will be destroyed.

Jerusalem will fall, again. The descendants of the hundreds of thousands of victims of Israeli aggression will want vengeance and payback, and Israel will, as a society, die. I also believe that when oil stops, so will this movement in Protestant Christianity, the apocalytes, the millions who prop up Israel in America, the Israeli Christian lobby. They are oil people, and when the oil dries up, they will move on. Unless there is radical political, economic and social reform in the Israeli state, the state of Israel will become another footnote in the history of the desert sands of Arabia and the land of the Patriarchs.

8.

DID JESUS
LIKE KILLING PEOPLE?

I have never fought in a war. I am not a soldier, but I have ministered to those who were, and are, and I have stood with them and their families, and always will. They are the forgotten people, useful sometimes, and then neglected. Tragically, most of the wars they have fought in could have been prevented, averted, or negotiated. Most died, were wounded, and scarred for life due to the stupidity, selfishness, and callousness of politicians and lobbyists. The majority of all soldiers, regardless of the flag under which they fight, do so with honor, are loved by their people, and are part of someone's family. Being a soldier is a profession. While the New Testament offers ethical teachings on this unusual profession, war is not consistent with Christian testimony, Christian living, and Christian faith.

This tension is an enduring one in the life of a Christian for there have been many Christian soldiers down through the centuries. Many have sought to reconcile their personal faith with their public profession. It is a difficult thing to do, and it is by no means clear, for them, for us, or for the Christian faith.

One example that comes to mind is that of General Charles Gordon (1833-1885), a man of interest to me, partly because of his loathing of institutional religion, but also his charismatic personal impact on those around him and his enduring influence on Britain and its foreign policy. I have been trying to track down contemporary accounts of his life for a series of novels I have begun, the first being 'The Curse of Crooked River,' set in 1872 about a man who served with Gordon, and who, like Gordon, struggles with the morality of being a soldier.

Gordon was a Christian, but not a typical one, and I am still researching his life and beliefs. Like most historical figures in the British Empire, he has been subject to revisionism, and his contribution jettisoned from history, or diminished. Gordon was unusual because his life as a soldier was against two false Messiahs, one Christian, the other Muslim. Both threatened stability, first in China, and then in the Middle East.

The first was Hong Xiuquan, a religious lunatic, and leader of the world's worst civil wars, the Taiping Rebellion (from the 1850s to early 1870s). The death toll was well over thirty million. Hong was a convert to Protestant Christianity, or one version of it, and simply created his own religion. It bears similarities to Christian Zionism in its simplicity but overall incoherence and inconsistency with the teachings of

Christ. Christian Zionism and the Taiping would share their love of killing people for the sake of Jesus, or their version of him. Both theological systems see the world as a titanic struggle of good versus evil, with no shades of grey. As a result, the Taiping engaged in brutality quite unlike anything the world had seen for centuries, and perhaps only in Pol Pot could a comparison be made.

Hong believed that he was the brother of Jesus, and engaged in mass murder and genocide, trying to force his own version of Christian 'communism' on China. The irony is that the Taiping Rebellion was the original menu of communist ideas and proposals that were taken up by Mao. Marx was not the primary inspiration for Marxism with 'Chinese characteristics.'

The Taiping were fundamentalists. Towns and villages that did not submit to his way of heaven were exterminated, men, women and children, all because of his twisted and sick version of Christianity. His theology was not that different from some European versions of the time, and much about his theology is obscured. He was too busy murdering people to write books about it, though he did write his own version of the Bible. The Taiping Rebellion is one reason for China's contemporary paranoia over foreign religions, and it is no wonder. Tragically, given the state of Western Christianity, the rise of another Hong is not inconceivable. If millions support Christian Zionism and MAGA, they will have no difficulty supporting a new version of Mr. Hong's Christianity.

The main difference between genuine faith and unhinged spirituality should be obvious and that is the deconstruction and application of ethical principles to other people made in the image of God. Those of genuine faith are people of love, or try to be, people of faith, or try to be, and people of compassion, or try to be. The vile, repulsive, disgusting rhetoric of Trump and his MAGA movement, the demonization of his political opponents into 'enemies within,' and his complicity and defense of the January 6, 2021, Capitol Hill riots is clearly associated with unhinged religious expression instead of genuine piety. This nonsense that America is falling apart, or in danger of being destroyed by Democrats and overrun by migrants is deeply sinful. America is the wealthiest nation in the world, one of the most powerful in the world, but perhaps that is God's curse on the wealthy and powerful, that with these blessings of the divine, the nation comes perilously close to religious mania of the most unhinged forms.

This tendency for religious insanity, America shares with China. Perhaps the only man capable of tackling religious insanity, fanaticism, and hysteria is another man of faith, one deeply troubled, deeply pious, and deeply respected by virtually everyone who met him or fought against him. We need more men like Gordon today in a world where fake religion, false piety, and unhinged political expression lift banners across the nation. Imagine that today, a Christian man, respected across-the-board, known for his personal integrity, his unwavering loyalty to his nation, but a man not afraid to step into danger, peril and certain death.

Gordon took command of the 'Ever-Victorious Regiment,' after the tragic death of the American adventurer, Frederick Townsend Ward in 1862. This regiment was a militia made up of Europeans and Chinese troops. After taking command in 1863, Gordon led the regiment in playing a decisive role in defeating the Taiping, also known as the 'God worshippers.' This militia won a string of over 30 engagements and fought alongside other brave regiments of Chinese troops from the declining, decrepit and corrupt central government of the Qing Dynasty (1636-1912). He refused all financial rewards and left China at the end of the war. Indeed, throughout his life, he was effectively incorruptible.

Gordon would later work for the British in Egypt from 1873 onwards. But his career, life, and Christian faith came to an abrupt and tragic end as a result of the decimation of an 8,000 strong British force sent to defeat an Arab uprising in 1883 by a man who called himself the Mahdi, a kind of Islamic leader. Gordon would go to Khartoum to protect British interests there, dying on January 26, 1885.

I mention Gordon because he was clearly a follower of Jesus, a most remarkable historical figure, and a soldier, someone who truly wrestled with the morality of war, and what it meant to be a Christian. History is full of such examples. The question I asked at the beginning, 'Does Jesus Like Killing People?' was one that Gordon and others like him would answer in the vein that Jesus was a man of peace, but that a man must do his duty for his country, even though in so doing, difficult choices need to be made.

The interesting difference between Gordon the soldier and others like him, and many Christians today who do not serve, is that for the latter group, killing others seems to be, something that God wants us to do. The idea is that Christians must support the genocide in Gaza, the war against Iran, and the invasion of Lebanon, all which involves the killing of many innocent people. The way so many civilians talk about war, killing, and murder, is disgusting, revolting, and morally repugnant. How quickly so many Christians deal out death and judgment to their enemies with their articles, their rhetoric, and their podcasts. Do they even know what they are saying? Are they aware that their inflammatory rhetoric is full of hate? Are they even cognizant that what they are saying is to promote a set of values that takes society back at least two thousand years?

Gordon would never have thought like this, and most Christian soldiers would agree with him today. This military sentiment is probably the result of the creation of modern armies, the end of the militias, better training, and the type of societies we live in today. Most soldiers in all armies, want peace, and are glad to come home, and look forward to the cessation of hostilities.

There are, of course, some soldiers and retired soldiers full of blood lust, wanting death in the Middle East, craving war and killing, but many of them want an online audience, they want a readership and are creating their online 'voice.' There are yet others who still work for the military industrial complex and they are bought and paid for operatives, and some have created their 'military' background in the same way some men pretended to serve in World War 2.

Why is that ideologies like Christian Zionism have problem with killing? Why is that Christians of all people, seem to eagerly support every action of war their nation pursues and cheers on every action of the Israeli Defense Force as if they were watching the Superbowl? Tragically, it is not new, sadly it is a Christian tradition, and repulsively, it happened soon after the life, the death, and the resurrection of Jesus.

It wasn't long before the followers of Jesus started killing each other. The early disputes in the New

Testament were over matters such as the cutting of the male foreskin, whether to eat food blessed at temples, whether to gather in the Temple courts or not, who oversaw various gatherings, and what the teachings of Christ were. If we accept that the boundaries between the 'followers of the Way,' and the synagogues (established by the Pharisees) were blurred until 70 A.D. when Rome destroyed Jerusalem, and this is a fair assumption, then the persecution Jesus spoke of enveloped the life of that first generation, those who saw Jesus in the flesh, or saw him in a vision. It is evident in the New Testament that some believed that Jesus was the fulfilment of ancient prophecy and that he was, in a sense, someone compatible with the teachings of the Torah and the prophets. This tradition is recorded in the Acts of the Apostles, and in some of the letters of Paul, and certainly is a theme in the gospels. This remains the orthodox, or most common view in Christianity today, that Jesus is the Messiah, the promised one, the anointed one of God, that he is the Jewish Messiah for the whole world.

The teachings of Jesus and that of this new movement were not accepted by many in the Jewish faith and there was conflict. This conflict resulted in the deaths of several Christians at the hands of Jews and Romans alike. But, by the fall of Jerusalem, the division was complete. This period covered about 37 years, give or take, as the years preceding the fall of Jerusalem were violent.

By the end of the first century, most of the writings we know as the New Testament had been composed and were being circulated around the communities in the region. Many people coming to faith in Jesus were not Jews. At this time, the second, third, and fourth generations of Christians were facing persecution from Rome and her emissaries, though for some time, Rome assumed Christians were a sect of Judaism. They were on the backfoot, hunted, and hidden, much many Christian communities today around the world.

By the time of Constantine's conversion in 312 A.D., things were about to turn around, as Christianity effectively became the church and it became part of the state, part of the Roman Empire as its official religion. This means there was two and a half centuries of persecution until Christianity, or a version of it, became Roman law. As an aside, the origins of our legal system come not from Christianity or Judaism, but an amalgam based on Roman Law mixed with some Christian principles.

Faithfulness before Constantine was shown by martyrdom and resistance, and faithfulness afterwards for many was shown by their ascetic ideals and desire to go into the desert and away from society. In other words, the true Christian either ended up dead or inflicted pain on their own person, two extremes of personal action and personal decision that really had nothing to do with God.

Christianity from about 312 A.D. or so, really began to be tangled up with the state, first the Roman Empire, then the Roman Church, then following the various schisms, the threads of Orthodoxy stemming from the Byzantine Empire, and following the Reformation, various national churches.

There was little freedom of religious thought in the past. Loyalty to the states today was preceded by centuries of loyalty to the church, with hideous punishments for disobedience. It was only in the period of capitalism, the middle of the nineteenth century in the Anglo-Saxon nations, and in parts of Western Europe, that we see the rise of free expressions of Christianity, as anyone daring to be free in the past were killed by the church, persecuted or banished. That is only about 150 years or so. Capitalism was the only system to facilitate some degree of genuine spiritual freedom. Many of those who call for a return to the West's 'Christian' roots, want a return to the days of religious tyranny, for that it what it was like.

I believe we are entering the end of this remarkable period of the free expression of the Christian faith, and the end of personal Christianity, and individual faith, and it will, once again be taken over by the state. Christianity will either be banned or controlled, but the days of freedom are almost over, dusk has come, and darkness is falling.

I believe that throughout these periods, there were many genuine followers of Jesus in various places, in various contexts, though not as many as have been thought. Most people in the East and West are and were cultural Christians and most will be in the future. Faith will be subordinate to nationalism and tied to nationalist projects.

The contradiction of capitalism is that while it has transformed our understanding of sin, and our understanding of church, within this period, there has been a remarkable degree of freedom, unlike anything we have seen in two thousand years, perhaps longer. These days, Christians do not need to go to church, and they can follow Jesus in their own way, and esteem him in their own manner. Whenever others say, 'you must go to church,' this is a relic or a throwback to the time of religious states when church attendance was mandatory, and when certain churches were approved, and others were not.

It was only in the period of capitalism that the

poor started attending church services. Before that, they were not welcome, and the ruling class didn't care about their spiritual or economic well-being. Pew-rentals were common, there were separate churches for servants, and most churches were for wealthy people, certainly the old ones. The poor were turned away from churches as they were filthy and unregenerate.

The idea that 'Christians always went to church,' is not true. You also see this idea of 'your Sunday Best,' when you dress up and go to church. Again, this is a throwback to the past, when the poor in the nineteenth century and early twentieth century would put on their only good clothes and go to church or to Mass. Wesley (1703-1791) was condemned by the Church of England for preaching outside of the church building to where the people were. These people, the poor, were hated by the church establishment. It is the same with George Whitfield (1714-1770) who was condemned strongly by many Christians for daring to leave the church and preach the good news to the poor.

The future of Christianity will be a renewed nationalist version of Christianity. We already see this in America. To be Christian means to support the state, even if your politics does not, you must be an advocate for America's wars and must be patriotic. In Russia, Christians must be orthodox. In China, Christians must join a state-approved church. India is fast becoming a Hindu state, and Christianity will possibly be banned entirely or restricted as it is in many Islamic nations. If Christianity is obedient to Western governments and their support of WW3, then those churches can exist. Pressure will be brought to bear on churches that do not support war, and I am sure loyalty tests are soon to be introduced. In other words, churches must sign up to the new war against China, as they have in the war against Russia.

Those who want capitalism to end in the church are usually those who want the church to have the sword once more, and when they get it, the killing will begin in earnest.

War has been terrible for faith. Not only is war a sin, but it has wreaked havoc on spirituality. It may come as a surprise to some that it is difficult to tell others about the love of Jesus at the end of a gun or talking to them after you have destroyed their home and killed their children.

WW1 led to a radical collapse in Christianity as Christian nations butchered each other. In Germany, the church rallied around the Nazi Party, and around Mussolini in Italy. After WW2, Christianity continued to decline, only to revive slightly due to the Cold War, but it has been in decline ever since. Copycat Christianity has emerged in India, and Africa, and elsewhere, and most are clones or copies of Western traditions, and a kind 'West worship,' is common. Many of these converts seem to think that God is an American, and that Christianity is Western. Links are assumed between wealth, the West and the church. Whether any of these expressions of Christianity are genuine, who knows? I doubt it.

What I do know is that whenever there is a new war, most of the Christian church in the West lines up to support it. What I know is that whenever there is a new war, Christian ministers line up to condemn the enemy and call for the deaths. What I know is that whenever there is a new war, Christians line up to forfeit their love, in exchange for hate.

Someone told me recently that what I say in

Freedom Matters Today reminds them of the writings of C.H. Spurgeon the Baptist pastor from the nineteenth century, and he also spoke about the need for authentic faith, that going to church didn't make one a Christian, and that being a Christian was about life, not ritual. I could not agree more with this sentiment. I drenched myself in the writings of Spurgeon in my youth and read and studied hundreds of his sermons. I also read A.W Tozer, J. C. Ryle, and some of the Puritans like John Owen and Thomas Brooks, as well as the famous Catholic writer Thomas Merton, and the Japanese author, Uchimura Kanzo. I stand with these men and their way of thinking about the need for an authentic faith. I speak to the generation of today, trying to show people the necessity of approaching the whole of life from a Christian perspective. For me, true spiritual freedom is knowing Jesus Christ, deepening my understanding of his spirituality, authenticity, and identity on the path of true freedom which comes from God.

Tragically, it is a minority view, as most Christians will support fascism, or Christian Nationalism, or Christian Zionism, or National Christianity without question, without criticism, and without regret, and most will not see that faith has anything more to do than a weekly ritual to be performed in a church, chapel, or cathedral Most do so with a clear conscience, for they neither think, nor care about others, even though to be a Christian, they ought to think about others, even their enemies, as it was for his enemies, Christ came (Romans 5: 10).

As I said, Jesus doesn't like killing people, but sadly, many Christians do, and they simply do not see that they are spiritually blind to the things of God, which suggests that many of them, as Spurgeon,

Tozer, Ryle, Uchimura, and I would agree, are not followers of Jesus. They are Christians in name only, and that is it, Sunday Christians, Cultural Christians, nominal Christians, fake Christians. Their hearts are dead, their minds are closed, and their spirits, well, they are not of God, for if they were, they would lay down their arms, they would put aside their prejudice, they would cast away their hate and follow Jesus.

If I so offended God that he sent his only Son to earth to die for my sin, then who am I to condemn others for the same sin that condemned me and cost me my presence with the divine, my communion with God, and the truest friend of eternity? Why then, would I see others any different from the way I see myself, one in need of God's grace, one needing forgiveness, and one loved by God.

Does Jesus like killing people? Many soldiers over the centuries have struggled with balancing their duty and their personal faith, but many civilians today want to kill their enemies, which suggest that something is wrong with the way Christianity is evolving. We are entering the end of free, personal faith, and the return of nationalist, cultural Christianity, so enjoy your spiritual freedom, for it is coming to an end and many of your 'Christian' friends are behind it.

.

9.

IS THE FUTURE PARADISE, PERDITION, OR PURGATORY?

Let me introduce myself. I live in Australia and own property. I have a vegetable garden, and live in a quiet, pleasant, and safe town. Birds visit, such as herons, parrots, and magpies, the soil is rich and fertile, and almost everything grows well. The services and infrastructure of the city are very good, and the roads are well-made, the trains run on time (usually), and the health system, a mixture of private and public, is one of the best in the world. If I am ill, I can be attended to quickly by some of the best nursing and medical staff in the world. I am in my third career, the first being academia, the second being the priesthood, and the third being a writer and publisher. To date, I have published 14 books in the last two years, through online publishing, a new form of publishing that was invented only in 2007. From time to time, I go abroad, usually to my favorite nation of Japan where I spent ten years of my life. I travel by plane, and while it is a little expensive, it is safe and efficient. This form of transportation was really only affordable from the early 1980s.

What I am describing is a world familiar to most of my readers. I have two things to say about this. The first thing to say is that this is not paradise. There remain problems within this idyllic society, if that is what it is. The problems are systemic, structural, and unavoidable. There are problems of the mind, income distribution, and the inevitable trials of life, which our society accommodates but does not resolve.

Others believe that I ought to feel guilty about this world, this nation, this life, that it was the product of ill-gotten gain, that it was the result of what they call 'white privilege,' and 'white supremacy.' I should feel guilty for being alive, for having an opinion, and for living my life. I should hang my head in shame, walk around in sackcloth and ashes, and weep and cry as I live on stolen land, from an oppressed people.

This belief in 'white privilege' is a form of mental illness, it is a delusion, and it is common among wealthy, middle class, well-educated, white people. These apologists for this mass delusion are keeping their nice homes, their investments, their money, and spend their time trying to make other people feel guilty about being alive. They are trying to create a secular theology, with a new set of sins, for a people made in their own image. The new set of 'social sins' are all about promoting division, and fragmenting identity, having us question our common humanity so they exploit, control, and abuse us, lying to us that we have nothing in common, cannot understand each other, and have no common destiny.

Sin is real, but being white is not a sin, owning property is not a sin, and living in this nation is not a sin. This delusion is a sickness of the mind, and these people are to be pitied and encouraged to find medical help for they earnestly need it. I believe it is one of the illnesses of prosperity, the sense of guilt that comes from success, the feeling of self-loathing that comes from the end of poverty, and that essentially what it is, is the failure to accept prosperity and to enjoy the fruit of capitalism as it exists today.

As I said, this is not paradise, and it never will be. We live in a capitalist society, and one of the great thinkers of the past, the atheist Karl Marx, talked about alienation, where workers and capitalists alike were alienated. One of the causes of class conflict was the inevitable dissatisfaction with what is, and the elusive nature of what can be. From my understanding of melancholy from Asian thinking, such as the poetry of Matsu Basho and others, is that this dissatisfaction is to be accepted and embraced as it simply suggests the transience of life, and the in evitability of death.

In our society, we believe we have conquered decline, we can do away with melancholy, we can feed alienation with other things, and we can pretend that all our problems don't exist. More recently, this has morphed in narcissism of the human body, the belief that we can overcome death by keeping ourselves in the peak physical form, from which we derive all our sense of self-worth.

The problem is that we are, above all people on earth, prosperous, and yet we believe the lie, that what we see is what will remain, that what we built will not topple, and that what we say is remembered.

Prosperity gave us so much and yet there is so much to do, and so much to attain, and so much to discover. Prosperity gave us a new liqueur to taste, a new tonic to ingest, a new draught to imbibe and drink we did. We drink deeply from this draught, and we tell ourselves that our world will live forever, that our problems can be postponed, that we don't need the divine, for we are living the paradise here, now, and that money is the answer to everything. But it is not true. We have been deceived.

It is the poison of paradise, the lie of capitalism, the deceit of prosperity. Capitalism is like a leech that sucks life from the soul of a person so all the goodness inside is drained leaving only dry bones. It is simply another lie of diabolos, from his menu which he has curated, crafted, and collected for humanity. We are just tasting the latest meal, and like the apple in Eden, it looks good to taste, it provokes the senses, but it is bitter.

America is but a puppet of the schemer of the world. As he dangles for us various promises like worms to fish in the pool, he does so to nations. We see the bait, but we do not see the hook, and soon, it is too late. We are caught in his snare, and we are dragged under, to the depths. For nations, there is no escaping diabolos, their future is dust, but for people, there is always hope, and diabolos has no control over the kingdom of God.

The sin of America, and its undoing, is greed, the most basic of lusts. America to retain economic power it must maintain greed. The original plan was to build global institutions that would provide rules of behavior and conduct. It worked well. The problem is that it worked too well, for other countries took America at its word, they accepted the rules-based

FROM THE JORDAN TO THE SEA

system, and believed that America was different, and
could be trusted. These other nations rose out of
misery into prosperity, began to think for themselves,
and wanted their own place in the sun, thankful to
America that it was beneficent, magnanimous, and
generous. We know now that this was a lie, it was
fake, it was an illusion.

American imperialism is just like British
imperialism. It will not tolerate the sharing of global
power. It is irresistibly addicted to absolute power,
and if other nations do not bow in humble adoration
before Washington, they will be destroyed. Russia
and China were tolerated if satisfying the American
market was their chief purpose in life. Trade was not
about building peace, but meeting market
requirements. There were positive byproducts of this
economic relationship. The Russian and Chinese
wealthy grew in power, and their middle-classes
flourished.

What of Britain? Britain could not control Europe,
so they left with Brexit and now they are tied to the
American imperialist project, but they want a piece of
the pie. They still are a major weapons manufacturing
center. Britian, once the world's power, is now a
lackey of America, always present, always ambitious,
always obedient, but Britain no longer holds real
power. Like America, Britain appears whenever there
is conflict, advancing the economic interests of the
British state. That's it. It is not about democracy or
freedom, but strategic interests and following
America. Even though they lost their empire, Britain
still longs for the glory of the past.

The endgame of American imperialism was that
this amiable capitalism would lead to peaceful
coexistence between Russia, China, and America.

Russia took America at its word. The Russian elites believed in the goodwill of the United States. The Chinese Communist Party also accepted the American overtures towards cooperation, and peace. It was called China's Peaceful Rise.

It was, to put simply, a trap.

America's deceit was perhaps the greatest strategic, decisive, imperialist action in centuries, to lure potential future competitors into unfair economic relationships where they could be controlled. If they sought freedom, they would be destroyed. We are seeing this play out in Ukraine and Russia right now, and will see it play out in Taiwan.

Through this rules-based order, America created an imperialist network that was their version of British imperial preferences that propped up the British Empire. America created its own economic empire in much the same way, using the rules-based system to ensure obedience, loyalty, and complicity. Their reliance on the American market would be their undoing, the means of their manipulation, and the mechanism for their demise. Europe, Japan, Australia, China, Russia, were among the powers in this imperialist net. Japan has a fake democracy, and Europe is run by the bureaucrats. They all pretend to believe in 'democracy' and 'freedom,' but they are not free. Democracy today simply means 'loyal to America.' It has no other meaning.

Behind this rules-based order was a specific political objective. The goal was to use economic power to effect political revolutions in Russia and China, to overturn political traditions, and put in place pro-American political leadership. This would ensure continual American economic prosperity.

America tried to topple Russia through Yeltsin. His

pro-American advisors and their policies bankrupted the nation. The myth of the fall of Russia was that Russian socialism was the cause of the collapse. It wasn't. It was the application of economic policies that were never implemented in the West. It was the free market myth. The free market has never existed in American capitalism, but Russia bought the propaganda hook, line and sinker.

The idea was that war could be prevented because economic power would transform political power. The belief was that democracy would rise from economic freedom, but it didn't because it doesn't. Democracy did not rise in the West due to economic freedom. Democracy rose as a mechanism to stifle revolution in the messy division of wealth in an imperialist system. Democracy was not a product of economic growth, but it was a device to legitimize the accumulation of wealth and greed. True democracy, the idea of one person one vote, did not occur in America until the 1960s. Within a decade, America was in trouble. American capitalism was in danger of collapse. A decade later, America cleverly brought Russia and China under its control through trade and investment and for a while, this new approach seemed to work.

The problem is that capitalism is merciless because it draws strength from human creativity. Capitalism takes the goodness of the soul, and it is transformed into commodities. But capitalism is not owned by America. It has a mind of its own and has no master. Like a tiger that tastes blood for the first time, Russia and China tasted the fruit of capitalism, and it was sweet, like honey, and they wanted more. They saw American prosperity and wanted it for themselves. They can create wealth and continue their political traditions. Russia will always have a strong leader. China will always have a one-party state.

They are both capitalist nations. They will not bow to America, and so America will happily provoke World War 3 to create a world with its own face. The goal of America since 9/11 has been to reshape the world so it becomes the singular political and economic power in the world for centuries. It is to create a world with an American face. Most Western Christians are onboard with this agenda for they believe that God is on the side of America, but that is not how it works. The devil is the prince of this world. Politics is his domain. He has a method, a scheme, a strategy, for these are the tools of his trade. It is the opposite to God. God is abundant, profligate, overflowing, indiscriminate. God's approach to the world is like a waterfall. The approach of diabolos is like a chessboard.

Capitalism is the current system. It will fail eventually. It will be replaced by something else. The new model will have a new façade, but the same principle, it will have new mechanics, but the same energy, and it will have new opportunities but the same problems. Capitalism is not the kingdom of God, nor was feudalism. The Kingdom of God is the presence, the power, and the person of Jesus. In every system, those who follow Jesus have struggled to find the balance of faith and life, and this is the journey for all people, working it out for themselves how to live in freedom, in a world that stands against God.

But the power behind America, is not God but diabolos and his promise is poison. The façade of America are its millions of Christians. Many of these Christians work well for diabolos, creating the myth of a Christian society, one that is driven by greed.

Greed is opposed to Christian virtue and the Spirit of God. Jesus said, a man cannot serve both God and money, but without American prosperity, there would be no American Christianity. Remember the words of Jesus, the one millions of American Christians claim to follow,

'No one can serve two masters. Either you will hate the one and love the other, or you will be devoted to the one and despise the other. You cannot serve both God and money.' (Matthew 6: 24).

What does this have to do with Israel. Everything. America needs oil to destroy China and Russia. Israel is America's puppet. If America can destroy Iran, then with Saudi Arabia, it controls most of the oil in the Middle East, and it can launch a long-term war against China and Russia, a war that will envelop the world in death.

Take a good look at the missiles falling on Israel. That is the future of the West, for it is not immune from destruction, it is not protected by God, it is not outside of human agency. What is happening in Israel and Iran will happen in America, in Britain, in Australia, in Japan, everywhere.

And on the sidelines, sitting in his comfortable chair, from his vantage point, the architect of war, diabolos, says to his puppets, 'Well done, good and faithful slaves, take the cup of paradise I promised you.'

This cup may have a great taste for a moment, but it is poison, and it leads to death. These days, most Christians call for war and thus out themselves as servants of diabolos, not Christ. To desire the death of others for whom Christ came, to desire the death of others made in the image of God, to desire the death of others, who are loved by God, is not the desire of a person who follows Jesus. Jesus came to bring peace, love, joy, and hope. Jesus did not come to bring war, death, suffering and misery. The tragedy is that these wars not only kill people but kill the gospel of peace, they disgrace the Prince of Peace and extinguish the proclamation of peace.

10.

WHAT IS THE LOGIC OF REVENGE?

The events of October 7, 2023, reminded me of a book written by Emeritus Professor Gary Trompf, from the University of Sydney. He taught 'Religious Studies,' that seemed to be a relic of the ancient practice of reading divinity at university. It was tucked away in an old, dusty, dark building, so maybe the university had forgotten about them. It happens. His seminal work was on the people of Melanesia. One of his books was titled, 'Payback, the Logic of Retribution in Melanesian Culture.'

Deeply ingrained in Melanesian culture was, and remains today, reciprocity. There are two parts. First, giving to others what they could not possibly reciprocate. This is the heart of hospitality in Melanesia. You do not give to receive; you give to place another in your debt. The second part is retribution. When someone you love is murdered, you do not kill the murderer, but you kill the one most precious in their life – wife, husband, or children. Then the survivors will do the same to you, and so on, until everyone is dead.

Read the accounts of this violence online. Now and then in Papua, it is played out in real-time, the most horrid crimes committed by ordinary people during a time of grief. Despite a century of Christian teaching, the logic of retribution and the impossibility of forgiveness is deeply rooted in contemporary Papuan society.

Trompf then thought about applying this thinking more broadly around the world. He found a similar logic exists in other contexts. It is easy to see the current conflict in this light.

I believe that all nations existed like this in the past, and most do today. This is true also for individuals, families, and communities. It is the law that prevents retribution in most nation-states, both modern and pre-modern, and there are severe penalties for the violation of these laws. Without these laws, there would be anarchy.

The logic of revenge is deeply rooted in the minds and hearts of many, for whom there is no forgiveness, only blood. It is for this reason that the law, and the police exist to keep us safe, keep us sober, and keep us sanguine.

Most Western societies believed in the logic of revenge, and it is still a deep memory in our minds. We see it played out in movies when the goodie kills the baddie and we breathe a sigh of relief. When we hear of a terrible crime, we expect the most severe punishment and lament the weak sentence.

But a competing idea emerged that challenged our natural thinking, our propensity for hate and our love of revenge. This came from Jesus of Nazareth, whom Christians called 'the Christ,' or Messiah. It was forgiveness. It was the idea that the actions of one man removed the desire for revenge. It was the idea that one man, who was killed by men who hated him, was able to plant a seed of hope in the world, an alternative to an endless cycle of death.

This cycle of death is the logic of retribution. It is deep, it is part of our DNA, it is our default setting. There is no end, there is no peace, there is only death. The point of brutality is not to kill someone, but to destroy those who are kept alive, to deprive them of their humanity, and thus, win.

Most of us did not know anything about Moses until the time of Christ. Throughout what became Western civilization from the 300s until today, these ancient ideas competed for the hearts and minds of nations. It was, and is, forgiveness versus retribution. Often, retribution won the day, but over time, the Christian idea of forgiveness, of finding some way to absorb the pain in oneself instead of lashing out, or seeking revenge, came to the fore.

For Christians, the logic of retribution died at the cross when Jesus died. Jesus did not say do to others what you would have them do to you. Moses said that. Jesus gave his disciples a new commandment: to love one another as he loved them. The life and death of Jesus was to be the model for others, not our hearts. Our standards were replaced by the standards of Christ, a life of service, sacrifice, and love. Even at the cross, Jesus said 'Father, forgive them, for they do not know what they are doing.'

Moses taught vengeance and revenge, blood for

blood, and a life for a life. This is an inescapable reading of the Torah, cities of refuge, the absence of forgiveness for intentional sin, and death for the violation of several commandments.

The Torah was not unique. It was a Hebrew spin on contemporary laws and beliefs. In other words, the Hebrews were not the only ones with that kind of legal system, but the Hebrews were the only ones who lived in covenant with Yahweh. Their laws, while strict and arbitrary were to be obeyed by a people whom God had shown mercy. Mercy existed under Moses, and there was even a tradition that stood against the rigor and inflexible justice of God in Deuteronomy that God would take revenge, and his people should rest in this divine expectation.

For some strange reason, many Christians believe that the Law of Moses defines the life of a Christian, but they are wrong. Christ taught us to love others, as he loved us, which is a life of self-denial, a life of giving, and a life of sacrifice for all, even for our enemies.

Christians are not to go out and take revenge. Christians get angry like everyone else, even fury and rage, and deep pain, but it is the Spirit of God who restrains us and reminds us of the consequences of our actions. This is why I question the authenticity of the faith of many who willfully embrace payback over long periods of time.

It is natural to want revenge, but over time, the Christian is supposed to be someone who would be content to let justice take its course. This is the power of forgiveness.

The events of the past week remind me that Christianity is largely absent in that part of the world, a world of land, history, faith, and violence.

For those who follow Christ, ours is a burden of love, because God shouldered his burden of love for us. Paul wrote in Romans chapter 5, verses 6 to 10:

'You see, at just the right time, when we were still powerless, Christ died for the ungodly. Very rarely will anyone die for a righteous person, though for a good person, someone might possibly dare to die. But God demonstrates his own love for us in this: While we were still sinners, Christ died for us. Since we have now been justified by his blood, how much more shall we be saved from God's wrath through him! For if, while we were God's enemies, we were reconciled to him through the death of his Son, how much more, having been reconciled, shall we be saved through his life!'

We were once the enemies of God, we stood against him, and yet, at this time, God chose to show mercy, and the greatest love. Jesus himself said in Matthew 5, verses 43 to 47:

'You have heard that it was said, 'Love your neighbor, and hate your enemy.' But I tell you, love your enemies and pray for those who persecute you, that you may be children of your Father in heaven. He causes his sun to rise on the evil and the good and sends rain on the righteous and the unrighteous. If you love those who love you, what reward will you get? Are not even the tax collectors doing that? And if you greet only your own people, what are you doing more than others? Do not even pagans do that? Be perfect, therefore, as your heavenly Father is perfect.'

These are difficult words, but life is lived at its best when the path is not easy. I would say with absolute confidence you have not lived until you have something awful to forgive, and there, it is between you and God. There is pain to forgiveness, there is loss, but how can we claim to love God if our standard is the same as the atheist who denies his existence and yet shows compassion?

What will happen in the Middle East? This logic of forgiveness and love is all that separates the West from the rest. Aside from this, we are the same. There is no logic of forgiveness in the Middle East, or parts of Europe, or Asia, or Japan, or China. There is only blood, vengeance, and retribution.

The result of the last week will be more death, more blood, and more killing, until either both sides decide to stop killing or there is no one left to kill. Enough blood has been spilt in this part of the world for several hundred years of retribution. Get ready for it. Indeed, the heart of this week's events is retribution, revenge, and payback.

What is the heart of the Christian message? The heart of the Christian message is that God killed the Messiah, his Messiah so that we might be free, a death on behalf of others, who, are by no means perfect.

The law of Moses taught that there was no forgiveness without the shedding of blood, and the blood that was shed for us, was the blood of Jesus. Hebrews 9: 22 says:

> 'In fact, the law requires that nearly everything be cleansed with blood, and without the shedding of blood, there is no forgiveness.'

The necessity for blood was at the heart of the teachings of Moses, so it was not just simply, love, love, love, but blood was required to pay for sin, both against God, and against others. Whatever you might think of Moses, he understood the misery and consequences of human sin, and he knew about blood. It must be paid.

We in the West have forgotten about the ancient logic of retribution, and we despair and wonder why they don't just forgive and forget.

Well, we don't, and we refuse to believe that our sins are so great that we need someone to die on our behalf. We believe that we are good enough for God, we are good people, and God is lucky to know us, and he is our father, and we are his children, but we fail to love others as he loved us, and in so doing, we prove that we are not his disciples.

11.

DOES GOD APPROVE
OF PALESTINIAN DEATHS?

One of the problems Christians face today is in applying their faith to the world around them. For faith to be real, it must start at home, and I am not talking about going to church on Sunday. I am talking about our relationships with others, our family, those whom we love, our friends, associates, work colleagues, and those whom we encounter in everyday life.

It is in these conversations, these encounters, these decisions, these actions within this small group of people which really defines, expresses, and proclaims the kind of faith we have, the sort of values we hold, and the character of the God we claim to follow.

Do you pray? Do you bring God into your conversation with those whom you love? Do you seek to be the best person you can, not because this will get you something, but because God is watching, and he knows everything. What do your children think of your faith? Do they pray and if they pray, do they understand what they are doing? Are you, in your little circle, your assembly of friends, being a witness to God and his Son Jesus Christ, or are you a closed book?

How can we make sense of Jesus? Looking back, we make sense of Jesus because others made sense of him, or he made sense to them, and they wrote about him. They distilled what they thought the people around them might find useful, helpful, and illuminating. These days, we can record all that we say and do, but in those days, they could not. John tells us that Jesus did far more and said a lot more than is recorded in the Bible.

That is not surprising. We have the condensed version, we have the best quotes, we have the most remembered encounters. Much of what we have is copies in triplicate, recorded in three versions of the life and ministry of Jesus Christ. We have the gospel of John, a very different book, in style, substance, and spirituality. We have the letters of Paul, John and Peter, and one from James, and Hebrews, whose author is lost to us.

These letters were copied and copied and many thousands of fragments of these letters and gospels remain today. These copies, fragments, and letters, form the corpus or basis for our New Testament. These fragments, letters and parchments survived through the centuries in various places. Soon, the teachings of Jesus became politically incorrect, became inconvenient, became inconsistent with the political version of Christianity promoted by the church within the European city states they now controlled.

The truth about Jesus became a political problem. They happily kept the Bible in Latin because no one understood it and this was a good thing, because the moment anyone opened the Bible, and read it, they would discover that the church lied constantly about God, the Son of God, and the life Christians are to lead. The truth about God was lost, the life about God was denied, the way to God was closed. For centuries, the Spirit of God moved in the hearts of people drawing them to Christ, and the church was there to kill them.

I truly believe that the Spirit of God has never stopped moving amongst his people, even though the church has done its best to stop him. He worked through men and women, shrouded by tradition, drowning in ritual and confused by language, by pointing them back to the Bible, to the words of God, and to the life of Jesus Christ.

One of the great moments in Western Christianity was the coming of the Bible in the local language, a repudiation of the official church text, a rejection of church authority, a retreat from church tradition. The men who did this, were murdered by the church, and eventually, the Protestants decided that their spiritual reformation would be based primarily on a Bible, on what the Bible said, on what it expected, and how it spoke to them about who God was, why Jesus came, and what he did.

A readable Bible became a threat to power. This was the turning point for Christianity. A Bible they could read, a text they could understand, and a God who seemed very interest in speaking clearly to them about himself, themselves, and others.

Until recently, Catholics kept their Bible closed.

The Roman Catholic Church until the 1960s sought to destroy the Protestant faith by murdering as many as they could, and they did not support the Bible in the local language until that time. There have been since then, a number of great Catholic thinkers, but they cannot, on the whole, disentangle themselves from church tradition, rituals and the hocus pocus of the Mass. Their theology is a dead end because it does not allow God to speak outside of their traditions, their rituals and their laws. The Pope is the boss, priests are special people, and people should pray to Mary.

The letter to the Hebrews is the antidote to the nonsense of Catholic theology that is stuck in a system that does not allow God to speak. There is nothing wrong with traditions, we all have them, but the starting point and the end point of understanding the Bible must be the text of the Bible itself. If tradition is wrong, then it should be discarded, or given lower status in the life of faith.

The Catholics are still emerging out of the Middle Ages. They are stuck in tradition, in the quagmire of Papal teaching, and the inconsistency between the vast wealth of the church, and the poverty of Christ. The Russian orthodox church is a church about which I said little. They too, are on a journey out of darkness, but a very different kind, a Communist one, and they are groping in the dark, in a perilous world, amongst a deeply traumatized nation. I leave them in the capable and wonderful hands of God.

The Protestants also have a problem with their theology. Their tendency is to get themselves tied up in knots, unable to move, unable to speak, and unable to change. Unlike Catholics, whose problem is located in tradition, and the orthodox in Russia who suffer deep trauma going back a century, Protestants pick up on a theme from the Bible to explain the current situation, but this theme becomes a stumbling block for them, and the more they seek to define it and defend it, the more it twists and turns them inside out, to the point where this theological system collapses.

The fall of Southern Calvinism was due to the slavery question. Southern Calvinism was the spiritual backbone to the Southern states that supported slavery and the institution of slavery. They took the doctrine of predestination, that God has chosen people from the beginning to be his people, and somehow, they took from this the idea that God had ordained some to be slaves and some to be free. The theologians of the South held that the Africans were slaves, and this had been ordained by God, and it could not change.

Critics would say that the Bible does not condemn slavery. I agree, but nor does it condone it. Slavery in the ancient world was commonplace, it was not racially bound, anyone could be a slave. Point taken. But the early Americans went to war against the Barbary Corsairs, the north African pirates in two sea-based wars. These pirates sought human cargo, especially Europeans, for sale in Africa. The Americans opposed this and fought against white slavery. According to Southern Calvinism, this was a sin, and the American government should have let the pirates take as many white people into slavery as they could, after all, God ordains slavery. Strangely, it was only black slavery he ordained.

Southern Calvinism never recovered from the Civil War, and most who hold to it today, cannot escape the historical problem of African slavery in the American tradition. This theological system was stuck and could not accommodate a God who loved all equally, who had no favorites, and who died for all, regardless of the color of their skin. The Civil War remains unresolved in America mainly because of the failure of Christians to embrace the Christ of the scriptures, to listen to the Spirit who moves across all creation, and follow the Father, whom Christ saw worthy for his constant obedience.

The current situation in Israel is another example of a theological system invented by Protestants which cannot accommodate the God of the Bible. It is a creation of men and women, it is not especially Christian, and it does not flow from the scriptures, but from the vanity, imagination, and delusion of man. I do not say women, because only men would be stupid enough to invent such a theological system.

This system of belief is that the creation of the state of Israel in 1948 is the first sign of the End Times, and that what will happen next is written about in the Bible. It is the belief that God speaks about a clear, step by step path towards the plains of Armageddon where God's enemies will be defeated. Israel is on God's side, Russia and Iran are doing the bidding of diabolos and America has been appointed to defend Israel against all evil. What is happening is of no importance except that it all points to the clear Rapture of all believers which will happen soon.

Let me be perfectly clear. This theological system prevents any humane discussion of the conflict in Palestine, it prevents any compassion for the suffering of the innocent, and it also teaches that genuine faith in Christ can also mean obedience to and submission to Satan. Many Palestinians are Christians, many Arabs are Christians, many Iranians are Christians, many Russians are Christians, but according to this theology, none of this matters because the Bible teaches this clear step by step program to the end of the world.

The problem is it doesn't. It is complete and utter, unbelievable rubbish. Every theological tradition invented by the American church has been shown to be complete and utter rubbish because they cannot disentangle faith and flag.

I am not talking about the Founding Fathers. That was and is a pragmatic political project. The Constitution is the product of many people thinking about the kind of society they want America to be, and in many ways, this document continues to shape the character, shape, and future of America. I would not call it a Christian document, but it certainly was influenced by men who called themselves Christians.

Too much theology means too little compassion. America's enemies are, according to this Israel-centric view, God's enemies. Iran, Russia, the Arab states, China, they all feature in this fictitious make believe of America's 'End of Days' scenario. All of these nations are the enemies of America or were at one stage in the recent past. How convenient it is that the Bible so clearly agrees that everything America does is according to God's will and revealed purpose in the scriptures. Not even the British were this arrogant, not even the Spanish under Franco.

Foreign policy aside, this theology traps Israel as much as it does the followers of Jesus. Israel did not become a nation in 1948. Israel has always been a nation, from Israel to now, or if you don't accept the historicity of Israel, Jacob, then from the Exile until now. Israel, whether in the promised land or out of it, did not cease to be a nation. The diaspora, spread across the world are the people of the Torah, the people of the Law and the Prophets, whether they live in America, Russia or Israel.

'End-Times' theology is dead-end thinking. In Revelation, the word 'nation' is mentioned 22 times and every time it refers to the nations, where we get our word, 'Gentiles' though this word is incorrect. Israel is mentioned 3 times, and none refer to the present time. Jerusalem is mentioned 4 times and, in every case, it is speaking of the New Jerusalem, the one that all of God's people will inhabit when Christ returns. Where are these specific references to the popular Protestant theological system that neatly packs the step-by-step process to the battle of Armageddon? It is not there.

These liars who make a lot of money from lying to people about the Bible, then go to the Hebrew Bible and to obscure passages like Ezekiel 38, where they allege, falsely, that Russia is Gog and Magog, the enemies of God. These liars don't even bother to do proper Biblical exegesis, they are so convinced, so full of their own self-importance, and so full of the expectation that they will get your money, that they don't bother even doing the hard yards to work out if it makes any sense.

Christ will return and that's the end of it. Christ will return. He will return when we least expect it. His return will be sudden and swift, and we can look forward to the New Jerusalem, a New Heavens and a New Earth.

In the meantime, anyone who calls on the name of the Lord shall be saved, anyone who calls Jesus Lord is part of God's family, and all made in the image of God, whether Israeli or Palestinian, or Arab, are those whom God loves, and has shown love, and especially, we believe, in the words, actions, and identity of Jesus.

I asked a question at the beginning: Does God

approve of Palestinian deaths? Most of these fake Christians would say, yes, he does, because if you stand against the state of Israel, then you stand against God, and since the state of Israel is central to the return of Jesus, those who seek to hurt Israel, or even question the policies of Israel in Palestine, are fighting against God and God's plan for humanity.

I have listened to so many of these liars and they will not even come out and say the words that Jesus said, 'blessed are the peacemakers for they shall be called Children of God,' (Matthew 5: 9). Might I also quote the Torah, 'you shall not commit murder,' or I might even go further and go to Deuteronomy, and say, 'vengeance is mine, I will repay,' says Yahweh.

I believe that the theological system that many American Christians hold will collapse as decisively as did Southern Calvinism in the past, as it cannot hold itself together. There are many brothers and sisters in Christ in Gaza, but according to these religious fascists, they are all the kin of Satan. How convenient a theology that writes their humanity out of existence, which denies their identity, and which says that because of some obscure theology, no compassion for them ought to be extended.

Does God welcome the death of innocent women and children? Does God laugh at the calamity of the nations when the missiles fall onto hospitals, schools, playgrounds, and churches? Is the life of one Israeli worth more in God's sight than the life of one Palestinian? If you answer yes to any of these three questions, I am sorry, I am truly sorry, but it is probably too late for you.

God is not on the side of genocide. The missiles that fly into Gaza are not engraved with the words 'From God with love.' This is man's doing, and man is responsible for it. It is, like all wars, sordid and sinful, and blaming God for it, or arguing that God is one anyone's side is a sin. God never takes sides in war. Wars are the result of human desires to have what is not ours, and to seek what we do not have.

The insistence of churches to 'Stand with Israel' is also a sin against God, for we are called to tell others about the good news of Jesus, not to promote war, enlist in conflict, or take sides in a complicated, historical mess that the West created and continues to shape for its own sinful interests.

There are legitimate grievances on both sides. This is a war of vengeance and revenge, in a culture of vendetta and blood, where the future is shaped by the past, which is an endless cycle of violence. The only future is forgiveness or total death.

Forget 'End-Times' theology, follow Jesus instead. I have shown that the most popular Protestant theological system to offer blanket and open support for Israel in Palestine is not Christian, not Biblical, and not coherent, in other words, it does not make sense. Whether you want to take a side or not, that is your choice, but if you do, then all wars must be short, and a bad peace is better than a good war, and war must be conducted with compassion, and soldiers must respect non-combatants, and all soldiers must fight with honor for God honors the day and nothing can escape his thought.

I have watched many of these guys on the internet. They have hundreds of thousands of subscribers, they are all very wealthy people, they live well in America, they drive nice cars and have nice houses, and I am sure they are all looking forward to giving it all up when Jesus returns, and they have to spend eternity with the people they condemn daily on their programs. Do these guys want Jesus to return? Course not.

Have you ever met a poor American Christian celebrity? There is your answer. Do you think these liars have all the answers? They are laughing all the way to the bank with your money. They offer no compassion to the victims of war, they are blinded by their own prejudice, and they have no interest in talking about Jesus Christ.

The best way forward is to expand your circle of friends to those with whom you disagree, and pray for them, walk with them, share with them your faith and your life. Put the fake theology aside, open the Bible, and rediscover the truth about God, forget the rambling, hateful speech of these liars, and follow Jesus instead. For God loves all he made, he cares for all who live, and he expects us to walk with all made in his image.

12.

OUR STRUGGLE

One of the vilest, most awful texts ever composed by a man was, for over a decade, the most popular, most-loved book in pre-war Germany. From its initial publication in 1925, it quickly became the book that couples would be given at their marriage ceremonies, everyone knew of it, most had read it, and it was undoubtedly one of the key devices for the effective rise of the Nazi Party.

The idea that Germans did not know what Hitler had planned for the Jews is a lie. I still hear it today from fascists. They knew. Hitler told them. It was in his book, titled 'My Struggle.' In this scribal obscenity, Hitler lays out his ideology and plans for exterminating Jews very carefully and cleverly. In fact, his rise to power surfed on the wave of unrelenting Anti-Semitism in Germany, facilitated in part by the Lutheran national church, which was deeply anti-Jewish and had been since it was founded. Martin Luther indeed had said many wonderful things about faith in Christ when he was not hating Jews.

I encountered 'My Struggle,' while researching my book on the rise of fascism, which is currently being prepared for publication. I didn't want to read it, but I needed to find a few quotes. I was comforted by the fact that my edition of the book had a preface written by a Jewish journalist who had fled Hitler in the 1930s and I reasoned that if this Holocaust survivor had opened its pages, then I could as well. I knew that by opening this book, I would be stepping into filth, for that is what fascism in all its forms is – pure filth. Fascism is the great evil of human creation. There can be no compromise with it.

The book's preface was a sufficient framework to use to navigate the bile, hatred, and frenzied vitriol against Jews and I trod carefully, knowing that I was reading a book that helped to cause the murder of over six million Jews along with homosexuals, masons, gypsies, and opponents of the Third Reich. I trod cautiously as I did not want to unsettle the dead, who were led like lambs to the slaughter, and whose bones were burned, scattered, and tossed like garbage. As a Christian and follower of Jesus, and deeply aware of the church's appalling relationship with Judaism over the centuries, I walked with deep respect, in silence, for the unforgotten dead.

What I found astonished me. I was speechless. Three things struck me. First, I could find no quote for my book that satisfied me, for Hitler did not stay on one subject long enough for me to find one. How his book was popular amongst the German ruling class of the 1930s was astounding. It was not that Hitler invented Anti-Semitism, it was already there, it was knee-deep, it was ingrained in German culture. As a piece of literature, it was almost impossible to read, and I could not read beyond a few paragraphs here and there before giving up.

The second thing that struck me was that Hitler was not mad, but a very clever, manipulative, and cunning person, for what he did was strip a human being of all their rich complexity, their variety, and nuances, and influences, to create a person in his image so he could murder them. That person was his definition of a 'Jew.' This was classic European Anti-Semitism.

Alfred Marshall, the father of neoclassical economics did the same with the discipline of economics in the nineteenth century. Economics before Marshall included history, culture, and politics, even class (Adam Smith and David Ricardo accepted the notion of 'class'), but Marshall disposed of all of them in favor of economic science. He stripped humanity of richness, culture, subtlety, and value to create the 'economic man,' what economists call the 'individual.' Some call Marshall's economic genius 'methodological individualism.' Marshall created the individual to pretend that economics was a science, which it isn't, but his intentions were not nefarious.

Hitler's goal, however, was to create a definition of a Jewish person so that their removal from society would not be noticed, or lamented, for everything they were, everything they believed in, and everything they said opposed German culture. They were, in Hitler's definition, against Germany, they undermined German values and what it meant to be German. That was his goal. It was largely achieved in 6 years when he took over and few Germans opposed the persecution and then extermination of Jews.

Even today, the grandchildren of fascists lie to my face and say that only a tiny group of SS officers knew what was going on. Tragically, and astoundingly, I have been hearing it more and more, and that is the argument from people seeking to defend Hitler and the Nazis in their so-called 'struggle' against Jews.

The third thing that struck me when I opened Mein Kampf was that Hitler sounded very familiar. I had heard him before. In fact, I had heard him a lot growing up in Australia. He is on the radio every morning, with the radio personalities who have the people they hate, the people they blame for the problems in society. Hitler is in parliament and on the voices of politicians who tell me that we have too many foreigners or too many refugees.

Most disturbingly of all, he is in the pulpit of many of our churches. Yes, Hitler is there too. In fact, he is experiencing a revival in the West in thousands of pulpits across many nations. Some people, mainly academics, don't know what it is, and so they call it the wrong thing. They call it Christian nationalism, but they are wrong. There is nothing wrong with flag-waving or loving your nation. We should call this religious cancer its proper name in honor of its true father, its true allegiance, and its true origin. It is Christian Fascism, or Fascism in the name of Christianity.

Maybe you are a Christian Fascist. Certainly, if you go to church in America or Australia or Canada or New Zealand or Great Britain, chances are you might be, or you may have come under the influence of a Christian Fascist, or read their books, listened to their sermons, read their online posts. I would guess that most church-going people in the West today are either Christian Fascists or people with deep sympathies for the beliefs, ideals, and values of Christian Fascism.

When Christians give up on Christ, they become fascists, every time. It is not surprising, since fascism comes from national Christianity. It didn't just appear in the 1920s out of the blue. Sadly, many simply cannot tell the difference between Christianity and Fascism anymore; the lines have been so blurred. If you are not a Christian, the response to fascism might be war, the process of steady destruction through aerial bombardment and missiles. It worked last time, and seems to be working in Ukraine, but at a terrible cost. No one truly wins in war, and it is not the war Christians ought to be involved. Ours is a spiritual war, not a physical war.

The Western Church is truly fascist for they are denouncing Russian intervention in Ukraine but will fall silent when the war is over and will say nothing. They don't believe in a spiritual war unless the government tells them to promote it, and they will keep their Bible closed until they are told by the state to open it.

I am a Christian and war is a sin, all wars, and that includes the War on Terror and the Twenty Years War in the Middle East. It is fascinating to hear Christians say that they don't want any assets tied up with Russia because war is evil, but they have assets tied up in America, and there is no greater warmongering nation than America. This is Christian Fascism at work. They don't know the difference anymore. They are such dreadful hypocrites.

So, to Christian Fascists I say this, you will not listen to me, but you will have to listen to God and his word the Bible. Fascism is a sin, and I hope that you will see it and recoil in horror, turn back to God and follow Jesus. If in the process, your entire world falls so be it, because what does it profit a person if they gain the whole world and yet lose their soul? There is no place in the kingdom of God for fascists, they wouldn't want to be there anyway.

Hitler was wrong. Fascism is always wrong. The Bible says little about liberalism and a little about socialism – we are free to choose the politics – but fascism is always, everywhere condemned. It has many names and takes many forms, but it has one father. His name is Diabolos. Remember him, fascists? His watermark is on lots of sermons now, his fingerprints in many pulpits, and his language in many churches.

All I can do, as a Christian is to remind you of the Bible, and for those of you who are not Christians or have been hurt by Christian fascists, know this: you are not alone, and not all Christians stand with the church, and not all Christians stand with fascists. Many Christians simply follow Jesus, or that is their goal each day as their life is a relationship with God, not a ritual, theirs is a faith, not a religion, and for them, God is big, he is real, and he can be known by anyone, and he has no favorites. God doesn't care about your church attendance, he doesn't care about your morals crusade, or your culture war, but he cases about his son, and whether you follow him.

I am sure that many of you have never heard these words from Paul the apostle. Certainly, the church will try to hide it from you, as these words oppose everything they say, and they need to say it because fascism brings in the money and they can live the good life while they keep the Bible closed and you are ignorant. It comes from Ephesians 6: 12:

'For our struggle is not against flesh and blood, but against the rulers, against the authorities, against the powers of this dark world and against the spiritual forces of evil in the heavenly realms.

13.

INTO ETERNITY

The New Testament teaches that we are eternal beings. The miracle of humanity is that we are all touched by the divine, and bear in our person the image of God, who revealed himself to those in the ancient past. It was this God who endowed us with reason and a conscience so we might weigh what is wrong and what is right. Everyone knows, in this elemental way, what comes from God and what does not, and most people today believe in a moral order whether or not they believe it is divinely inspired or a product of human creation.

Recently, I had an argument with a few people over age, what we know call ageism, because in the West, age is hated, despised and loathed, and the youth are worshipped, adored, and revered. It is why churches have youth groups and Sunday schools and are   obsessed   with   Christian   schools   or homeschooling. Yet, as people age, their faith evaporates because we do not believe in eternity, we do not believe that we are eternal beings, because we believe the lie, that image is all that matters, that the future is in the hands of the youth. Is it any wonder that leaders such Mr. Putin is so popular today when he points out the fundamental moral weaknesses in the West. He is right. The West has lost its way. The fundamental belief in right and wrong has been replaced by new laws and new morality such as ageism, such as the worship of youth, the idea that we are useless the older we become, and that truth only resides in those closest to the womb.

We have in the West created the society Pol Pot, Stalin and Mao so eagerly desired, a world without the influence of age. We did it voluntarily, with enthusiasm. With age comes experience, wisdom, and maturity, but as we prepare for war with China, the caution of the older generations is dismissed in favor of the fanaticism of youth. We believe that it will be different this time. This time we will win the war, destroy our enemies, and prevail. Yet if we meet anyone old, they will tell us, no, it is folly, it is stupidity, it is foolishness, for with age comes pain, with age comes experience, and we glimpse eternity, for we are eternal beings. But as youth, we do not see eternity. All we see is the here and the now, and when the bombs fall, even that will be taken away.

We must all give an account of our lives before God, which means what we do in this life matters, what we say matters, and how we live, matters and when we stand before God, what will we say to him, and how will we account for our moments, our days and our nights?

We are eternal beings which means we live

forever. The Christian teaching involves the proposition that we can know God through knowing the person, the power, and the presence of God in Jesus, the Messiah. As we can know him, we can know God, and the image endowed in us from the beginning can shine more brightly as God reveals in our hearts love, peace, and joy. The reason why so many Christians support war is that they don't believe in eternity, they believe the lie of diabolos that land, flag, territory and nations matter. They don't. All that matters is to know God and by knowing him, know ourselves, and in knowing ourselves, we can reach out to others with the love that God extended to us in the person of Jesus. But I don't believe many Christians today know anything about God, for they love war, they delight in conflict, and they can tolerate the suffering of others.

As eternal beings, we are all accountable and moral creatures and as such we know when we have crossed the line, we know when we have done wrong, we know when we have strayed from the path of goodness. I believe that God is a merciful and a forgiving God and he extends his hands of forgiveness to all who truly turn back to him who recognize what they have done is wrong, and desire to live a new life under the authority of God and his Son, Jesus Christ.

I believe that Jesus came to die for the sin of the world, and that by his death he brought true life into the world. This means that no one is too far gone to be beyond the love of God, that no one is too deep in despair to be beyond the kindness of God, that no one is too wicked or evil to be beyond the mercy of God.

In the horrors of war, I see hope, not only the hope of peace, but the hope of lives and hearts transformed, that people who despise and hate each other might, because of God's love, reach out to each other in human fellowship, from the river to the Sea, from the Jordan to the Sea, from Washington to Iran from Sydney to Beijing, there is nothing too impossible for God, there is nothing too difficult for God, there is nothing too overwhelming for God. If we can do it, then it is not a miracle, but we know the God of miracles and I believe in peace, I believe in transformed lives and I believe in forgiveness and love, for without love, we have nothing.

We are eternal beings because we serve an eternal God. While he is present in war, it grieves him as do all wars, as his creation fights in his name, but not with his Spirit. We must find the road to peace, the road back to God, and the road back to humanity.

I believe in the God of revelation, not in the god of the soil. Jesus didn't come so we can worship at Jerusalem, but that all will worship the Father in spirit and in truth (John 4: 23). What God has to say concerns us all. I believe that God cares very much for all of his people, and he grieves for his world, and what his people are doing to it, and to each other. He has seen nations come and go, peoples rise and fall, tribes form and decay. This period is no different. God holds us all to account, what we do with our lives, how we live them, and how we esteem him and his Son, Jesus.

For me, I do not see a future for the state of Israel if it continues on its current path. Christian Zionists will disagree and smugly point me to their complicated End-Times schedule in the allegorical book of Revelation, which is not meant to be taken literally. My answer is simple. There is no Rapture. You will have to live with the nightmarish world you are creating. You will be eternally accountable for your lack of love, your lack of compassion and for your lack of faith. Christian Zionists may have to pray to the God they pretend to believe in. You will reap what you sow, and you will spend eternity facing those whom you have condemned, opposed, and killed. Christian Zionists, if they are truly Christians, will need to explain to God why they sought the death of Palestinians as a prerequisite for the return of the Son of God and why they believed God was the author of sin. They will face eternal shame as they will spend eternity with those whom they murdered, persecuted, and condemned. What a fate for any person.

As for Israel, it seems to be the case, that providence has ordered the creation of nation-states, the way that all nations of the world today are formed. It would be odd, strange, and untenable for Israel not to go down this path. Their desire to create an ethnically pure society is fraught with all kinds of problems, not least the reality that it will continue to be a pariah in the world until certain, basic rights have been resolved for the Palestinian people.

As of October 2024, Israel is now attacking UN peacekeepers in Lebanon, and openly talking about extending new settlements in Gaza, effectively consigning two million people to a life of poverty, misery, and suffering. Children continue to die from war and from starvation, aided and abetted by America, Australia and its tiny group now, of allies. Israel is brazened, it is confident, it is a rogue state and a failed state, for all nations that fail to care for their people have achieved nothing. All states have failed in the past, many have recovered, and some are still in great trouble, especially in Africa. But Israel is among them, a failed state, and out of control.

If Israel continues along its path, it will expel all the Palestinians, Arabs, Muslims and Christians from their territory, creating a strange society, for it will be a society of only ethnic Jews, surrounded by nations who will not forget, and will not forgive. If Israel turns Gaza and the West Bank into a series of settlements for wealthy Jews from around the world, then, for the first time in centuries that most of the world's Jews will all be in one place, one vulnerable, little place in the middle of the Middle East, surrounded by nations that have had enough of them.

It would be a strategic blunder of immense significance because placing most of the Jewish people of the world in one place is not a good idea. It is an idea of incredible foolishness and could lay the basis for the third Holocaust, the first being the fall of Jerusalem in 587 B.C. and the second being Hitler's Holocaust. Remember, the Holocaust in Europe happened because all the Jews were in one place – Europe, and through their collaborators in Ukraine, Latvia, Estonia, Lithuania, Poland, and other countries, Jews could easily be located, rounded up and murdered. It was a Holocaust on an industrial scale possible only because of modern technology, organization, and logistics.

If the presence of Palestinians in the West Bank and Gaza have been, to date, reasons for restraint from Israel's enemies, their absence would answer that interesting question: would an ethnically pure Israel become a more likely target for aggression from the Arab world? Netanyahu seems to believe that mass murder and genocide will be forgotten and that the Middle East will band together and pursue economic prosperity with the Arab nations eagerly helping Israel in the future. Oh, how naïve he might be. Vengeance is not so easily dislodged from the human psyche.

An ethnically pure Israel is in a vulnerable strategic position, and it doesn't matter if it is protected by America and the Iron Dome. America might leave, and the Iron Dome is just another form of technology. Eventually, a weakness will be found and exploited. Creating an ethnically pure society is a regressive act of any state, especially one that claims to be democratic.

The only way forward is peace, through the creation of a state where all are welcome. If Israel decides to go down this path, it will met all the obstacles, difficulties and trials that other nations have faced, and overcome, for it would mean that a real nation would rise and be a light to all peoples. But now, it is a pariah, and its plan for an ethnically pure society would place Israel in a strategically vulnerable position, opening it up for potential national disaster.

I don't think the leadership in Israel can see anything other than Greater Israel, from the Jordan to the Sea, but this is not God's concern, nor is it God's mission for the world, nor is it the concern of any Christian. The Christian believes in the good news of Jesus, to the ends of the earth, that Jesus matters because he is the Son of God, that all people matter because they are made in God's image, and that the mission of Christians matters because it is one of peace, joy, and love. Soil is soil, but a person is not home until they know God, and the greatest promise of God is that he might be known, and the greatest fulfilment of that promise is the person, the presence and the power of God in Jesus.

ABOUT THE AUTHOR

Rev. Dr. Michael J. Sutton is the author of 15 books and is the CEO of Freedom Matters Today, looking at freedom from a Christian perspective. The goal of Freedom Matters Today is to equip, empower, and encourage you in your journey of faith, life and spirituality.

https://freedommatterstoday.com/

www.ingramcontent.com/pod-product-compliance
Lightning Source LLC
Chambersburg PA
CBHW070636030426
42337CB00020B/4035